Driven To Our Knees

Volume 2

Help For Those Struggling Through The Trials Of Life

By Vic Coleman

Driven To Our Knees – Volume 2
by Vic Coleman

Published by:
Victor Coleman
7544 FM 1960 Road East #1015
Humble, TX 77346

ISBN: 978-0-578-00430-3

Bible references are from the New International Version (NIV) unless otherwise noted.

Scriptures quoted from *The Holy Bible, New Century Version*, copyright   1987,1988, 1991 by Word Publishing, Dallas, Texas 75234. Used by permission.

Scripture taken from the HOLY BIBLE, NEW INTERNATIONAL VERSION
Copyright © 1973, 1978, 1984 International Bible Society. Used by permission of Zondervan Bible Publishers

Scripture quotations taken from the Amplified® Bible, Copyright © 1954, 1958, 1962, 1964, 1965, 1987 by The Lockman Foundation. Used by permission. (www.Lockman.org)

Contact Information:

Vic Coleman ♦ 7544 FM 1960 Road East #1015 ♦ Humble, TX ♦ 77346 ♦ viccoleman@yahoo.com

Blog site: VicColeman.com

Table of Contents

Acknowledgements

I must first acknowledge my Lord and Savior, Jesus Christ, who, out of His goodness has saved my family and me. There is no life without Him. He *is* life.

Secondly, I must acknowledge my wife, Virginia. As with the first book, she has been my support; daily praying for me, encouraging me, and providing an occasional "get back to work" nudge.

As always, I'd like to acknowledge our sons, Lionel (LT) and Steve, my mother and all of our family and friends.

And finally, I'd like to acknowledge Pastor Carl A. Lucas, Sr. of God First Church in Spanish Lake, Missouri. He has been a true friend, providing correction, encouragement, spiritual covering, and much needed practical help.

Introduction

This book represents the second of the *Driven To Our Knees* series. Volume 2 represents "more of the same", i.e., practical, straight forward lessons that help bridge the gap between Scripture and the trial you or someone you know is facing. As with the first book, all of the lessons in Volume 2 are scripturally based, and derived from times when I was "driven to my knees". During those trials, I read my Bible more intensely in search of answers, encouragement, and a closer relationship with God. Typically as I read, a certain passage would catch my attention. I would read it over and over again, take notes, and meditate on it. The result was the next Bible study lesson for our home bible study group.

Through these lessons you will learn much about God and His ways. *The main goal of the book is for you to develop a deeper personal relationship with Him.* It is through this relationship that you will find the comfort, strength and encouragement you need to overcome *any* trial. I won't promise that you will receive the answer to every, "Why me?", but I do promise you that if you take time to read the Scriptures, mediate on His Word, and earnestly seek to know Him better, your life will radically change for the better. Your circumstances may or may not change, but you will change *inside*. The Holy Spirit will "renew" your mind and transform you in a way that will make you more like Christ. Others may notice the change in you before you do.

The Scriptures teach that God wants to "conform" us to the image of His Son; to transform us from the inside out. As this transformation progresses, you will begin to realize that overcoming any obstacle is possible because of Who is inside you.

And He Heard My Cry

Introduction

There are times in life when it seems that you are surrounded by trouble. It seems as though you're being attacked on several fronts – your job, finances, relatives, health, and personal weaknesses. And there seems to be no end in sight. You've cried out to the Lord, but He seems silent. You know that He's there because you can point to other things He's done for you in the past. But you wonder, "Where is He now? Did He hear my cry?"

One of the most significant events in the history of Israel was the Exodus from Egypt. The Bible refers to this event numerous times throughout the Old and New Testaments. As I thought about all God did in the lives of Israel during this time, it became clear to me that God hears our cries also – and performs miracles which confirm His presence. Some miracles are immediately obvious to us, but others we miss. A closer look at the events surrounding Israel's departure from Egypt will teach us much about how God operates in our lives.

Scriptures Used In This Lesson

Exodus 3:7 – 10

Exodus 3:19 – 22

Exodus 5:22 – 23; 6:1 – 8

Exodus 11:4 – 9

Exodus 13:17 – 22

Proverbs 3:5

Exodus 14:1 – 31

Genesis 50:24 – 25

Psalm 18:6

Background

The tiny nation of Israel came to Egypt during the time when Joseph was "second-in-command" under the Pharaoh (Gen. 46:1 – 7). They were welcomed at first and settled in the region of Goshen to avoid a severe famine that plagued much of the surrounding land. At that time, the nation consisted of about 70 people, Jacob (Israel), his wives, sons, daughters, daughter-in-laws and their children. Sometime after Joseph died, the Egyptians turned against them and put them in bondage.

As time passed, their numbers grew. Over the course of 400 years, they had grown from 70 to over 2 million people. The distrust and disdain of the Egyptians towards them grew as well. They were hated so much that the Egyptians tried to convince the Israelite midwives to kill baby boys as they were born (Exodus 1:15 – 22).

It's A Process: Step By Step

In their bondage and suffering, the Israelites cried out to the Lord. God heard their cry, but their deliverance did not come immediately. Read Exodus 3:7 – 10. In this passage, God acknowledged their suffering to Moses at the burning bush. He also said that He was "concerned" about their suffering (NIV). The KJV states that God said that He "knows their sorrows". "Knows" is translated from the Hebrew word "yada" which means to be acquainted with, to perceive and see. So God knew what they were feeling.

Key Point: God hears our cries the first time we sincerely call Him. He also knows what we are feeling and the full extent of the situation.

Moses would eventually go back to Egypt, confront Pharaoh several times, and perform many miracles, before Pharaoh freed the Israelites. There was a process to complete before deliverance would come. God had a specific purpose in mind in doing things the way He did. He revealed this purpose and what He would do step by step. And this is how He operates in our lives, fulfilling His purpose "step by step".

Key Point: God fulfills His purpose in our lives "step by step".

In the scriptures below, God revealed His plan and purposes:

- Exodus 3:19 – 22
- Exodus 5:22 – 23; 6:1 – 8
- Exodus 9:16 – 19 (God, through Moses, tells Pharaoh of His purpose)
- Exodus 11:4 – 9

Can you think of a time where you looked back at your life and realized God had been preparing you for something specific? Can you think of a time when you reflected back on your life, saw the hand of God, but did not see it at an earlier time? Why did you not see it earlier, i.e., what "clouded" your vision?

When you think about it, the "step by step" approach makes sense for God fulfilling His purpose in our lives. Are any of us born doctors or surgeons? No, we must take gradual steps before achieving these goals, i.e., attend kindergarten, elementary school, junior high, high school, college, med school, residency.

Something to think about: Life is a process, a series of steps.

After their release, God directed the Israelites to take a specific route to freedom. Read Exodus 13:17 – 18 for background. He knew His people. He knew what they were ready for and what they weren't. God led them away from the Philistines; He knew that the newly freed slaves were not ready for battle.

In the same way, God knows the battles for which we are ready. Some battles/trials we avoid. He prevents certain things from occurring or He leads us in an opposite direction. Other times, He sends us "into battle", but never alone or unprepared.

Key Point: If God allows something to happen in your life, He has prepared you or enabled you to overcome it. But you'll have to depend on *His* strength, not your own, and trust *Him* for the victory.

Key Point: There will be times when you won't understand the "Why's" of what you are going through; you will just have to make a decision to trust Him. Read Proverbs 3:5.

God's Words Come To Pass

There are many instances of God's Words coming to pass throughout the Bible, but Exodus 13:19 is a relevant example. Joseph, by inspiration from the Lord, foretold of this event 400 years earlier (Genesis 50:24 – 25). For us today, it provides more assurance that God's promises will come to pass, no matter how long it takes – 4 minutes, 4 days, 400 years. His Word is True. This truism provides us with the basis for comfort and freedom from worry.

Why do we struggle when it takes longer than we expect for God to deliver us? How do you feel as a parent when your children worry about things of which you've given them assurance, knowing that you have everything under control? How do you think God feels when we worry? How can we worry less?

He Will Never Leave Us

Exodus 13:20 – 22 highlight a very important point: The presence of God is always with us; He will never leave us nor forsake us. There was always the presence of God in front of His people. His presence as a "pillar of cloud" was actually visible for 40 years. Even in their disobedience, He never left them.

Key Point: God will never leave you.

Fulfilling His Purpose

In Exodus 14:1 – 4, God orchestrates the events to bring His purpose to pass – which is to glorify His name. Even the ungodly will know He is Lord. This is also how He works in our lives. He will work out the people and events in our lives so that only He will receive the glory. Many times we miss the fulfillment of His purpose because we respond to circumstances the wrong way. *We focus on and react to the bigness of our problem and not the bigness of our God.*

Exodus 14:5 – 12 illustrate our typical response. The chariots were real. Pharaoh not only included his regular chariots, but "six hundred of the best chariots" to pursue Israel. *All* of Pharaoh's horse and chariots, horsemen and troops pursued the Israelites and *overtook* them.

Verses 10 – 12 exemplify our typical response - fear, doubt, rebellion. The Israelites were on the verge of experiencing a fantastic miracle of God, but fear, doubt and rebellion were their responses. But God graciously ignored their reaction.

Key Point: Many times we miss a miracle of God because we respond the wrong way to our circumstances.

> *Have you ever felt like your problems and circumstances were going to overtake you?*
> *What are the "chariots" in your life and how do you typically respond to these "chariots"?*

In the midst of the storms of life, try to listen to the "lone voice of faith". In verses 13 – 14, we see that Moses was the "lone voice of faith" trying to encourage the fearful mass. I believe if we listen, we will hear the "voice of faith" (the Holy Spirit) speaking to us either through prayer, reading the Bible, or through the words of other people. We have to first take our eyes off of the "chariots".

Specific Instructions and Obedience

Typically, God will give us specific instructions on how to overcome our enemies (circumstances). It is our job to be obedient. Fortunately for Israel, Moses was obedient to God and Israel saw "the glory of the Lord".

Read Exodus 14:15 – 22. See how in verses 19 – 20, God protects His people. When God is for you, no one can stand against you.

Key Point: The keys to our victory, experiencing a miracle, and seeing God receiving glory are our obedience and faith.

The balance of the chapter tells how God delivered His people. Fortunately for them, He ignored their fear, doubt and rebellion.

Summary

Everyone experiences times when the "chariots" of life speed toward us to attack us. We may be out manned and out gunned, but this does not spell defeat. It simply places us in a position to experience a miracle of God.

**Keys To Victory
In The Life Of A Believer**

Three thousand years ago, David wrote these words of encouragement and assurance:

> In my distress I called to the LORD; I cried to my God for help. From his temple he heard my voice; my cry came before him, into his ears. (Psalm 18:6, NIV)

Your voice *is* heard.

Driven To Our Knees

Notes:

Notes:

How To Make God Mad

Introduction

During a recent time of personal study, a certain theme kept coming up. Over a period of two weeks as I read and listened to the books of Psalms, Matthew and Mark on CD, I noticed that there were certain things that angered our Heavenly Father. To my surprise (and dismay) I found myself doing those things quite often. It seemed so easy to fall into this particular "sin".

As we go through trials and tribulations, we eventually seek the Lord for help (the sooner the better) – this is a step in the right direction. But as times goes on, we often engage in activities that take us two steps backwards, thus nullifying our petitions to the Lord.

This lesson is a study in those activities that so easily entrap us and gets God mad.

Scriptures Used In This Lesson

Psalm 78:9 – 22

Exodus 16:1 – 8

Psalm 95:7 – 11

Matthew 16:1 – 12

Matthew 10:1

Forgetting The Past

A study of a passage in Psalm 78 provides some clues on getting God mad. The first section provides a summary of Israel's (referred to as Ephraim) sin. Read Psalm 78:9 – 11. We are told of three things:

1. They did not keep God's covenant
2. They refused to live by His law
3. They forgot what He had done for them

These three speak of the "faults" we constantly exhibit:

1. We do not live as if Christ is our Lord and we are in a covenant relationship with God through Christ. We accept Jesus as Savior, but His lordship is far from us. We don't live as if God is with us throughout the day. We rarely ask for guidance during the day or stop to ask for wisdom. Unfortunately, too often the first time we think about God during the day is when we sit down for our evening meal. We pray at meal time only as a result

of a habit developed during childhood, and not out of a true heartfelt desire to give Him thanks.

2. We refuse to live by God's laws and principles. Since Christ's lordship is not first in our lives, we do things on our own or to please others. Sometimes we "go with the flow" and little by little distance ourselves from the Lord. If everyone else is engaged in an activity, we follow along to be part of the group, so we won't be rejected at some level. We never stop to ask, "Is this godly conduct? Am I really living in a manner that is consistent with Christ, to the best of my abilities?"

3. We forget the things God did for us in the past. As soon as the current crisis is over and the pressure subsides, the "memory lapse" begins. We experience a time of "peace" and then the next trial occurs. The reality of what God did for us in the past is like a mist, it's there, but of no real substance; not relevant enough to encourage us for the current trial. *We don't carry the foundations of faith from the previous trial to the next.*

The last item is where I found myself the most lacking…I forget the past. I am thankful when the Lord delivers me through a trial, but by the time the next one comes about, I find myself "beggin' and pleadin'" as if I don't know if God *can* or *will* deliver me. This is what gets Him mad.

Read verses Psalm 78:12 – 16. Here we are given a list of things God had done for Israel.

> *What has the Lord done for you over the past year? Take a few moments to make a quick list. Were the things the Lord did for you significant? Did they affect your life or the life of others around you in a positive way? How often do you remind yourself of the things He's done? Why do we forget His goodness? Why do we continue to sin against Him?*

Next read Psalm 78:17 – 22. Verse 18 says that, "They willfully put God to the test…" (NIV). The KJV phases it this way, "And they tempted God in their heart…" The word "tempted" (or "test" in the NIV), comes from the word "nacah" which means to test, or to prove. So Israel was trying to make God prove Himself to them by demanding the food that they craved.

Now read Exodus 16:1 – 8 for background. What's interesting about the passage in Exodus is that Israel's vocal complaints were directed at Moses and Aaron, but the attitude of their hearts (which was disbelief) was directed towards God; He took it personally. After He had delivered Israel from Egypt in a great way, they doubted if He could provide them food. *They didn't carry the "foundation of faith" developed by the previous miracles forward to the next trial, which was hunger.* Instead of seeking the Lord (Who was visibly present in a pillar of fire or cloud every day) for food, and feeling confident because of what He did for them in the past, they doubted His willingness and ability to help them in this current situation. This is what got Him mad. Notice what Moses said in Exodus 16:8, their grumbling was not against him and Aaron, but against God.

Now back to Psalm 78. Verses 19 – 20 clearly present the doubt of the Israelites. But we are no different today. How many times has God delivered you in a great way, and a week later, you doubt if He will help you in the next trial. Verses 21 – 22 show how God responded to their doubt. We are told not only that He became angry, but *why* He became angry.

The attitude Israel displayed affected God to the extent that it is mentioned several times throughout the Bible. Psalm 95:7 – 11 is an example.

> *Why do you think God gets angry when we doubt Him? Assuming you are a loving parent who has provided for your children for several years, how would you feel if they doubted you? As a parent what would hurt you the most, the disbelief in your ability, the disbelief in your love, the disbelief in your intentions, or the disbelief in your character? Why? What do you think hurts God the most?*

Some Things Don't Change

A New Testament example of God's attitude towards lack of faith is found in Matthew 16:1 – 12. In the first part of this passage, Jesus has an encounter with the Pharisees and Sadducees. They wanted to "test" Jesus by getting Him to perform a miracle. The fact of the matter was that they had already witnessed or heard of several miracles; they just wanted to cause Him to "slip up" and undermine His popularity and influence.

Verse 5 tells us that the disciples forgot to bring bread with them on this trip. In verse 6 Jesus warns His disciples to be on guard against the "yeast of the Pharisees", referring to the encounter that just occurred. Verse 7 tells us that the disciples had concluded that Jesus made His comment because they forgot to bring bread so they could eat.

Now Jesus' response to their conversation was very revealing (verses 8 – 11). Instead of initially saying, "You all misunderstood me. I wasn't talking about food...", He begins by saying, "You of little faith...". Now why would the first thing out of Jesus' mouth be a criticism about their faith? The answer lies in Matthew 14 & 15, where the disciples had recently helped Jesus miraculously feed 9,000 people. With Jesus, food was not a problem; it should not have even been a topic of discussion. Their faith should have been at the level where they cared not about their needs – Jesus was with them. They should have immediately looked deeper into the meaning of Jesus' warning about the "yeast of the Pharisees".

As you read verses 8 – 11, you can sense a tone of frustration with the disciples, especially verse 11. Not only had the disciples participated in the feeding of 9,000 people, they had witnessed many other miracles. They had even gone out in pairs with the authority to "drive out evil spirits and to heal every disease and sickness." (Matthew 10:1). So given what they had personally experienced, they had no excuse for worrying over the bread they had forgotten. Their lack of faith is what got Jesus frustrated.

Why do you think the disciples were concerned over bread? What are you concerned about? Why? Given what you know God has done for you personally, should you be concerned? Why or why not?

Summary

The key point in this lesson is very simple and straight forward:

When God does something for you, carry that experience forward in your life; use it as a foundation to further build your faith in Him.

Faith in God goes beyond what He will do for you; faith in God is the basis for your relationship with Him. When a loving parent is not trusted by his/her children, the hurt cuts deep into their heart. This is especially true when the parent has "proven" himself/herself time and time again. That's what God feels; that's why He got angry with Israel. That's why Jesus got frustrated with His disciples. That might be the reason God is frustrated with you.

Make some time within the next 24 hours to do the following:
- Take a sheet of paper and fold it in half.
- On the left hand side, make list all things God has done for you in the past 12 months.
- On the right hand side, make a list of all of your current concerns.
- Make a decision to use the left side of the paper as your foundation of faith for the right side.
- Review the list every day for 30 days.
- When you pray (daily), begin your prayer thanking God for the things He has done on the left, and for taking care of the issues on the right.

After a while you will begin to realize that there is no reason to get Him mad; only reasons to rejoice.

Notes:

_____

_____

_____

_____

_____

_____

_____

_____

_____

_____

_____

_____

_____

_____

_____

_____

_____

_____

_____

_____

_____

_____

_____

_____

_____

_____

_____

_____

In The Belly

Introduction

As young children, we have all heard the story of Jonah. Some know his story as "Jonah and the Big Fish"; others know it as "Jonah and the Whale". We are all familiar with the basic story line that Jonah was told by the Lord to go to Nineveh. Jonah did not want to go and decided to get on a boat and sail to Tarshish instead. Along the way, a storm came which endangered the ship. Eventually Jonah was thrown overboard, and swallowed by a big fish, where he spent three days in the belly. Later he was "vomited on dry land" and went to Nineveh where his preaching caused the people to repent and turn to God.

As I read the book of Jonah, chapter 2 caught my attention. The entire chapter takes place inside the belly of the fish. As I thought about this scene, I realized that Jonah was at the lowest point in his life. He was helpless, caught in the grips of death, with no way out. When we are driven to our knees by life, we can find ourselves in a similar type of situation, where the only option seems to be "to give up".

Is there hope? Yes! As long as there is a God in Heaven, there is hope. This study focuses on Jonah's prayer and provides the evidence for our hope in the Lord.

Scriptures Used In This Lesson
Jonah 1
Jonah 2
Proverbs 6:16 – 19
II Samuel 21:15 – 17
Psalm 18:3 – 6, 16 – 19
Exodus 20:3 – 6
II Corinthians 5:18 – 21

What Is "In The Belly"?
Read Jonah 1:1 – 2, and 2:1. Jonah found himself inside the fish because he had sinned, i.e., he had deliberately disobeyed the command of the Lord. Jonah was in a dark inescapable place, most probably surrounded with partially digested food. The "belly" is the near-death experience. It can be physical, emotional or both. It is a point where we feel helpless, hopeless, and overrun by our circumstances. Similar to Jonah's experience, our "in the belly" experience will be dark, uncomfortable, distasteful, and all encompassing. We may feel that we have been "eaten alive" by our circumstances. Death may seem to be just a step away. We are "in the belly".

We feel that we have sunk as low as we can go; life can't get much worse. Read Jonah 2:3 – 5 to get a sense of how helpless Jonah felt.

Recently I was confronted with an experience that seemed like it was beyond me. Every step I took to try to correct the problem was unsuccessful. I found frustration around every corner. I asked for help from others, but they were limited in what they could do or the time they could give attending my needs. The clock was ticking away and I felt helpless. Several times in my mind I said, "I give up. I just give up. There's no way out."

> *Have you ever had an "in the belly" experience? If so, what area of your life did it affect? Have you seen others go through an "in the belly" experience? How did you/they survive?*

How do we get to this point? Many times, we find ourselves in difficult situations because of our decisions and acts of disobedience like Jonah. Sometimes these decisions can have very dire consequences, not only for us, but for others as well. We sit back and wonder, "How in the world did I ever get myself in this position?"

You may not experience your "in the belly" event immediately; it may come over time. Jonah didn't experience the fish until sometime after he traveled in the opposite direction of the place God instructed him to go. Read Jonah 1:1 – 3. Nineveh was near the Tigris River in northern Iraq; Tarshish was probably in Spain. The extent of Jonah intentional disobedience is more clear when we realize that Tarshish was about 2000 miles from Nineveh.

> *When was the last time you willingly disobeyed God, i.e., His laws, principles, or direct instructions? How did the circumstances initially turn out, pleasant or unpleasant? How did the circumstances turn out over time, pleasant or unpleasant? Did you encounter consequences that were for the most part, expected or unexpected? Did you benefit from disobedience? Why did you disobey? Why do people disobey, in general?*

Key Point: You can't run from God.

Key Point: Many times we will encounter *unexpected* consequences due to our disobedience to God.

Here is a list of the type of decisions that can get us into trouble, i.e., "in the belly":

- Willful disregard of direct instructions from God
- Disobedience of biblical principals
- Going contrary to sound wisdom
- Decisions based on rationalization (justification of actions after you've already decided to engage in them)
- Decisions based on manipulation (of circumstances, people, etc.)
- Decisions based on trying to win the approval of others
- "Spur-of-the-moment" decisions, or ones based on passion or rage/anger
- Any of the sins listed in Proverbs 6:16 – 19
- Fear
- Worry
- "Vain imaginations" (acting upon thoughts that you have imagined
- as if they were true)
- Bitterness

What type of decision got Jonah in trouble? What types of decisions get you in trouble? What type of decision do you think "trips up" most people? What is the best way to keep from falling "in the belly"?

Not all "in the belly" experiences are due to our decisions. Sometimes we are entrapped by our enemies − physical and spiritual. Read II Samuel 21:15 – 17. This "in the belly" experience of King David came when he was engaged in battle against the Philistines. He had fought until he was exhausted. Seeing his condition, one of the Philistines determined to kill him. But one of David's soldiers came to his rescue.

Can you think of a situation where someone may have been "in the belly" due to the actions of others? What about children abducted by others? What about soldiers engaged in a battle? What about those who get laid off from their jobs? What about those whose spouse or parents have abandoned them?

Sometimes what we experience is not our fault; things just happen over which we have no control.

Key Point: Sometimes bad things happen because we live in a sinful world that is separated from God's guiding Holy Spirit.

Your Cry Is Heard

Read Jonah 2:1 – 10. Let's take a closer look at what the Word is telling us. Verse 2: Even though Jonah was in this position because of his disobedience, and he felt that he was as low as he could go, the Lord still heard his cry. *For the child of God, there is no condition or situation that is out of reach of the hand of God.* He can hear your cry no matter what's going on. Jonah's cry was one of desperation, sincerity, intensity, and repentance; one of "I've got no where to turn except to the Lord."

Verses 3 – 5: These verses describe the severity of Jonah's condition. Notice the following phrases (from the NIV). Have you ever felt this way before?

- Hurled me into the deep...
- The very heart of the seas...
- Currents swirled about me...
- Waves and breakers swept over me...
- Engulfing waters threatened me...
- The deep surrounded me...
- Seaweed was wrapped around my head...
- To the roots of the mountains I sank down...
- The earth beneath barred me in forever...

Needless to say, Jonah felt he was in a hopeless condition with no way out. Things could not get much worse. Notice Jonah 2:6. Jonah felt "barred in forever", but the last half of the verse shows the hand of God. Again, it bears repeating, *there is no condition or situation that is out of reach of the hand of God.* Read Psalm 18:3 – 6, 16 – 19. David felt the same way, and came to the same conclusion: God heard his cry.

Key Point: For the child of God, there is no condition or situation that is out of reach of the hand of God. Your cry is heard.

Attitude Is Everything

A natural response to the Key Point above is, "Well why doesn't God do something...now? I'm suffering!" The key to Jonah's salvation from certain destruction is found in verse 7. His attitude towards the Lord was not one of anger, impatience, or frustration. It was one where he had given up, completely, and as he looked toward the Lord, his heart cried out. He had a repentant heart that acknowledged the holiness of God. *The Lord, not his circumstance, was his primary focus.* It was at this point that Jonah could be in "right relationship" with the Lord. His heart had turned, from one of disobedience to one of obedience. Jonah had repented.

In verse 7, Jonah "remembered" the Lord; he offered up a prayer to His "holy temple". In Jonah's distress he still recognized God as *holy* and honored the Lord as such.

> *When you were "in the belly", did you remember the Lord...as holy? Why or why not?*

Read verse 9. With a "song of _thanksgiving_", Jonah would "sacrifice" to the Lord. He acknowledged that "Salvation comes from the Lord". What's Jonah saying in all this? "God, I honor *You*." Jonah placed God <u>above</u> his circumstance.

Key Point: The key to our deliverance is placing God above our circumstance.

> *Have you placed God above your circumstance? Have you honored Him in spite of what surrounds you? How can we transition from "consumed with grief, regret and worry" to "consumed with the Lord"? What holds us back and keeps us from making that transition?*

What Are You Clinging To?
I skipped one verse in all this – verse 8. Read verse 8. This verse caught my attention more than any other.

> They that observe lying vanities, forsake their own mercy. (KJV)

> Those who cling to worthless idols forfeit the grace that could be theirs. (NIV)

> Those who pay regard to false, useless, and worthless idols forsake their own [Source of] mercy and loving-kindness. (Amplified)

> *What are you clinging to? What do you think will bring you deliverance and rescue you from your trouble? What have you been imagining? What is the focus of your hope...your perceived deliverance or God? Who is your savior, your bank balance or God? Who is the source of your strength (physical, emotional, and mental), yourself or God? Will satisfaction come from a new job or God, Who provides the right job?*

Key Point: Jonah's focus was on God, not his deliverance.

If we cling to our solutions, if we place our hope in other people, money, things of the world, or a relationship, we forfeit the favor of the Creator of the Universe – the One who spoke the world into existence. *Where you place your hope for deliverance becomes your idol. Emotionally and mentally clinging to the perceived solution to your problems, instead of the One Who provides your solution, is a rejection of Him.* It's almost like turning your back on Him and looking to something He created.

Key Point: Where you place your hope for deliverance becomes your idol.

Key Point: God said, "You shall have no other gods before me." (Exodus 20:3)

God wants to be the primary focus of your life. Nothing should be placed above him...not your spouse, child, money, career, deliverance...nothing. God wants you to know Him on an intimate level. The situation you're in now is an opportunity to draw closer to Him and to get in right relationship. You may have thought you were close before, but now you have the opportunity to get even closer. *Our focus in life must be Him, not what He can provide.*

Be Reconciled

Read II Corinthians 5:18 – 21. The word "reconciled" comes from the Greek word "katallasso" which means to "return to favor". God wants us to be "returned to His favor" through Christ. He wants us to be close to Him; to enjoy an intimacy beyond what we imagine – even in the midst of trials.

Human nature is one where we are motivated to change by discomfort. When a young child misbehaves, we sometimes apply a mild level of "discomfort" to his rear-end to "encourage" him to change his behavior. Adults, unfortunately, keep this same nature. The discomforts of life motivate us to change. God uses our discomfort to "katallasso" us and bring us to a new level of intimacy with Him. The key is in how we respond.

If we respond in anger, frustration, disobedience, bitterness, or despair, we lose the opportunity for deliverance. But if we give up and turn our heads towards His holy temple, as Jonah did, then He hears our cry. He will first act upon our hearts; that's where the intimacy takes place. Then He may or may not change our circumstances. But we will overcome through our trials by our intimacy with Him, and His Spirit renewing our hearts.

We can't make it on our own. It takes the grace of God to survive and thrive. That is why Jonah's words ring with truth:

"Those who pay regard to false, useless, and worthless idols forsake their own [Source of] mercy and loving-kindness. (Amplified Bible)

Summary

In your darkest hour, God is there. You are never alone. Jonah was inside a fish at sea, and God still heard His prayer. God will never leave you nor forsake you. But you must place Him first, above anyone, anything, and even your perceived source of deliverance from your trials. He will meet you wherever you are (even in the belly), hear your prayer, and act in your behalf.

Notes:

_____

_____

_____

_____

_____

_____

_____

_____

_____

_____

_____

_____

_____

_____

_____

_____

_____

_____

_____

_____

_____

_____

_____

_____

_____

_____

_____

_____

_____

Why Our Faith Doesn't Overcome

Introduction

Faith is the key to living successfully as a Christian. Especially when we are in the midst of trials and tribulations, faith in God can mean the difference between "makin' it" and "fallin' apart". Many times we fall because we fail to believe in God's abilities, His willingness to help us, or His ways.

This study focuses on the various reasons why our faith doesn't allow us to overcome our trials. My hope is that one or more of these will "stop you in your tracks", and you will say to yourself, "You know, that applies to me. Now what can I do to turn around?"

Scriptures Used In This Lesson

Hebrews 11:6

Acts 16:16 – 34

Proverbs 16:3 – 4

Proverbs 19:21

Joshua 1:5 – 9

Philippians 4:6 – 9

Romans 8:38 – 39

Romans 8:29

Mark 4:1 – 20

Luke 5:1 – 11

Luke 4:31 – 39

Isaiah 55:8 – 11, 12 – 13

The Object of Our Faith

Faith is a critical component in the life of a believer. The Bible tells us that without faith it is impossible to please God (Hebrews 11:6). But before we can please God, we must make sure that the object of our faith is correctly placed.

Back in grade school grammar classes, we learned that the object of a sentence was the thing that received the action. For example, in the sentence, "I ate the apple." the subject is "I", the verb or action is "ate", and the object, or the thing being eaten is "apple".

When we speak of "faith", we need to ask the question, "What is the object of my faith?", or, at the expense of proper grammar, "What's my faith in?" Too often we place our faith in the wrong thing. Our faith should be placed in the things that never change, and that's the character and nature of God. I specifically said the "character and nature" of God because sometimes we place our faith in how we want God to act in our behalf.

For example, read Acts 16:16 – 34, the account of Paul and Silas when they were preaching in Philippi, a city in a region currently known as Greece. In this passage you can see that "bad" things happened to Paul and Silas. They were:

- Falsely accused
- Rejected by large crowds of people
- Severely beaten
- Placed in the "inner prison", the worst of prison conditions
- Placed in stocks (Roman stocks were designed to cause pain in addition to limiting mobility)

Notice in verse 25, around midnight, they were singing praises to God. Now their faith was not in God's deliverance from "bad things", because "bad things" had already occurred. The object of their faith was in the character and very nature of God, not their circumstances. Their faith was in:

- God's sovereignty: no matter what happened, God was in control. His plan for them would be fulfilled. (Proverbs 16:3 – 4, Proverbs 19:21)

- God's faithfulness: no matter what happened, God would never leave nor forsake them. (One of my favorite scriptures contain the words of encouragement God gave to Joshua, Joshua 1:5 – 9, especially, verse 5).

- God's peace: The power of God's peace is what gave them the desire and ability to sing songs of praise in the midst of a "storm". (Philippians 4:6 – 9)

- God's love: They knew that no matter what man did to them, they would never be separated from God's love (Romans 8:38 – 39). They knew that God cared for them.

- God's power: God's power was great enough to overcome any set of circumstances, as evident in Acts 16:25 – 26.

Because the object of Paul and Silas' faith was "in the proper place", their mindset was such that they kept the Roman jailer from killing himself, and preached to his whole household, who later came to believe in Christ (Acts 16:27 – 34). You may wonder, "How could this be?" Well, faith, properly placed, can raise you *above* your circumstances. God receives glory as others watch His work in you. They will see that "the power is real"; He confirms His Word with power.

Do you know of someone whose faith allowed them to overcome tribulations? How or why did their faith overcome their trials? What effect did it have on others who were watching? What effect did it have on you? Do you think you could have overcome the trial like they did? Why or why not?

What Happened To The Seeds?

Now let's read Mark 4:1 – 20. Verses 1 – 9 tell the parable of the sower and the seeds. Starting in verse 14, Jesus gives us the interpretation of the parable, with the seed being the Word of God. Re-read verses 16 – 19. Jesus provides two reasons why believers don't overcome.

First, believers have no "root", meaning their relationship and understanding of God is very shallow. They may know John 3:16 and a couple of other scriptures, but their knowledge of the Word is not very deep. As a result, they don't know the character or ways of God. So when tribulations come their way, they fall back on what they know best – emotions, logic, influence of others, and fear. Their responses to trials resemble that of an unsaved person.

The solution: Study the Word of God on a regular basis. Pray and build your personal relationship with Him. Ask Him to show Himself to you in a way that will encourage you and build your faith.

The Object of Your Faith Should be Placed on the Character and Nature of God

Other People
My Strength
My Logic
My Faith
The Character and Nature of God
How I imagine the outcome I want will be obtained
My Current Circumstances

The second reason Jesus outlines why believers don't overcome is because they become consumed by the "cares of this world". Their daily focus is on their circumstances, troubles, comfort, and desires – everything else but God. Sometimes our lives start to revolve around the "stuff" that He provides, and not Him. We only come to God for what He can do for us, not for knowing Him as a Person. This would be like a child only going to their parent for "stuff" (selfish reasons). After a while the

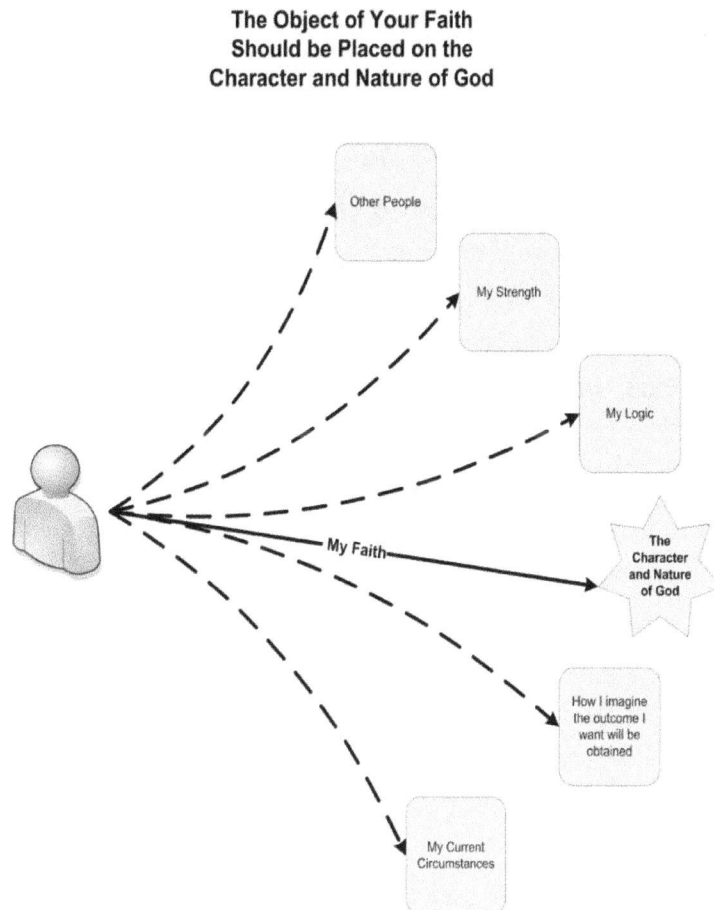

parent will feel rejected by his/her own child, and come to realize that the child may love "stuff" more than them. The parent may decide to take away some of the "stuff" to show the child what's more important, and to "weed out" the selfishness. (Has this happened to you?)

Has God removed something in your life to get your focus back on Him?

The solution: Study the Word of God on a regular basis. Pray and build your personal relationship with Him. Ask Him to show Himself to you in a way that will encourage you and build your faith.

The solutions are the same because they both lead to a Verse 20-type relationship with the Lord, one that's fruitful. God wants you to have a personal, one-on-one relationship with Him. All the "things" He provides are just "extra"; the relationship is priority.

One of the warmest relationships I've ever had was with my grandfather. Whenever I think about him, I just have a warm feeling inside. He was a good man. I don't remember if he ever gave me anything like toys and money and "stuff"; he probably couldn't afford it being a farmer in rural Mississippi. But while spending time with me as a child, and as he taught me to drive his tractor, he gave me something that I still carry to this day. I try to pattern myself after him so I can be a "good man" too.

This is similar to what the Lord wants from you. He wants you and He to be so close that you get a warm feeling inside when you think about Him. Your relationship should be such that you want to pattern yourself after Him, so that when people see you, they see Him. Read Romans 8:29.

Do you know someone who has become overwhelmed by their circumstances? What's been the effect on their faith, as they focused more and more on their circumstances? How can they be helped? What should they do? What should you do?

Key Point: Sometimes the pleasures of life can choke the "seed" just like the difficulties of life.

Key Point: A personal relationship with God is more important than "stuff". There is nothing wrong with "stuff"; it's just a matter of priorities.

Do you know someone who became focused on the pleasures of life? How did it affect their personal relationship with the Lord? Why?

It Seems Impractical

Read Luke 5:1 – 11. In this familiar passage, we see Jesus instructing Simon (Peter) to go out into the lake and cast his nets for a "catch". Peter, a fisherman, had been fishing all night and had caught nothing.

But he says in verse 5:

"…But because you say so, I will let down the nets." (NIV)

Don't Let "Stuff" Get Between You and Christ

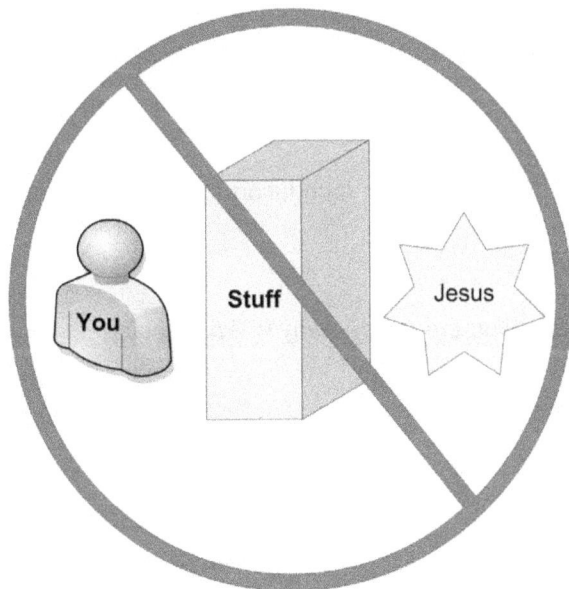

It's Bad For The Relationship

He did as Jesus instructed and caught more fish than he could handle.

Now Peter made his living as a fisherman; Jesus did not. Peter had been fishing all night long and had caught nothing; Jesus had not. Based on his professional skills, experience and logic, he could have easily told Jesus, "No." The justification to refuse to be obedient clearly presented itself to Peter. But he *chose* to be obedient, even though his obedience defied logic, i.e., it was not logical to fish at that time of day after fishing all night and catching nothing.

Peter's choice to be obedient was based on a belief in the power of Jesus. Read Luke 4:31 – 37. Here we see Jesus teaching, healing and casting out demons in an area near Peter's home town. Verse 36 says that news about Jesus spread throughout the surrounding area. Now read verses 38 – 39. Jesus heals Peter's own mother-in-law. So Peter witnessed a miracle first-hand. So his obedience in Luke 5 was based on his belief in Christ in Luke 4.

What's significant for us is that many times when it comes to believing the Word or something the Lord has laid upon our hearts, we choose not to act on it because it seems impractical, illogical, inconvenient, or contrary to common sense. *We don't use what God has done for us in the past as a foundation for faith in our current situation.*

In a sense we are like Peter, in that we can point to things God has done for us in the past that "defied logic". But right now, we don't believe because of:

- our experience and knowledge
- our assessment of our skills
- the opinion of other people
- our logic (actually based on limited knowledge of the facts)
- fear or uncertainty
- other emotions
- our mental picture of the situation
- it's something we don't want to do
- it's inconvenient

As a result, we miss out on a "great catch".

Key Point: We don't use what God has done for us in the past as a foundation for our faith in our current situation.

Which one of the above reasons seems to affect you the most? Why? What should you do about it?

The solution: Document what God has done for you in the past and review the list weekly. This will build your faith and keep God in a "dominate" position in your mind, instead of your circumstances. Then as always - study the Word of God on a regular basis. Pray and build your personal relationship with Him. Ask Him to show Himself to you in a way that will encourage you and build your faith.

A Few Other Reasons

There are several other reasons why our faith doesn't overcome. To name a few they are:

- Bad teaching or no teaching. We believe wrong things about God and His ways.
- What we heard is something we don't want to do, believe or hear.

Other Reasons Our Faith Doesn't Overcome

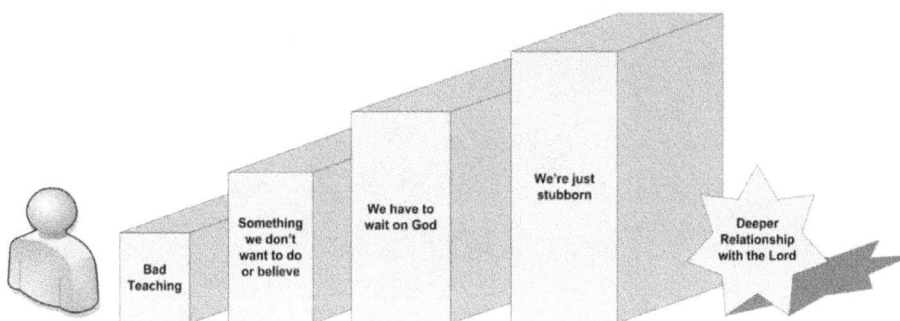

- We have to wait on God.
- We're just stubborn in releasing our preconceived ideas.

All of these things keep us from developing a deeper relationship with the Lord by hindering our faith. Hindered faith leads to defeat instead of victory.

A Word About Faith

Throughout the New Testament, "faith" comes from the Greek word "pistis", which means in part:

1. *conviction of the truth of anything, belief*
2. the conviction that God exists and is the creator and ruler of all things,
3. *belief with the predominate idea of trust* (or confidence) whether in God or in Christ, springing from faith in the same
4. *fidelity, faithfulness*
   a. *the character of one who can be relied on*

(Emphasis is mine)

Faith is not the same as hope, as in "I hope God helps me". It is a conviction and a trust. With the ways of God being so far above us, we usually don't have a clue as to the details of how God will act in our behalf. We just know that He will. As a reminder read Isaiah 55:8 – 11.

Summary

Faith that overcomes is the privilege of every believer in Christ. We have a God who can do anything, at anytime, in anyway. We stumble because of various reasons as outlined in this lesson. But the solution is the same for all of the "stumbling blocks" – a growing, deep, personal relationship with God, through Jesus Christ, by the power of the Holy Spirit. As our relationship grows, we will stumble less often, and will even be able to help others in their walk of faith.

Sometimes we get discouraged because things don't turn out the way we expected or wanted, or the trials seem to go on and on. But we must remember what the Scriptures teach. Re-read Isaiah 55:8

– 11, but this time continue to read through verse 13. As your relationship with Him grows, "you will go out in joy and be led forth in peace". Don't try to figure it out, just trust in His divine character and nature. You will overcome, because His Word, which dwells in you, is powerful and effective.

Notes:

Are You Ready To Sing?

Introduction

There are times in our lives when the trials of life emotionally overcome us, especially when one "bad" thing happens after another. It seems like "we just can't get a break." Our spiritual vision becomes so clouded that we don't even feel like looking up to God, much less praying to Him. We go to church and the songs seem so empty. We wonder, "Really...where is God?"

This lesson focuses on a series of events in the lives of the apostle Paul and Silas. As they were preaching, they encountered a number of severe trials that should have had them screaming in agony to the top of their lungs. But yet they sang, and their deliverance came "rubblin' in". See what we can learn about Paul and Silas so we can bring in our deliverance - "singing our way to victory".

Scriptures Used in This Lesson

Acts 16:16 – 34
Luke 4:31 – 37
I Corinthians 3:16 – 17
John 14:16
John 16:13
James 5:16
2 Corinthians 1:3 – 4

Just Minding Their Own Business

Paul, Silas, Luke and Timothy were in the city of Philippi, in a part of the world called Macedonia, during Paul's second missionary trip. Philippi is located in Greece, along the coast of the Aegean Sea, north and west of Athens. It had been a Roman colony for a little over 100 years and was a prosperous city because of near-by gold mines. The year was about 49 or 50 AD.

Paul and Silas were preaching in the city when they encountered a slave girl who was a fortune-teller by a demonic spirit. Read Acts 16:16 – 18. In verse 18, the KJV says that Paul was "grieved" by the girl. The word comes from a Greek word "diaponeomai" which means that they were troubled, offended, and pained by this girl. Today we would say, "She was extremely annoying and getting on their nerves, big time." So Paul commanded the spirit to leave her.

After the evil spirit left the girl, a series of events occurred that spelled trouble for Paul and Silas. Read Acts 16:19 – 24. If we detail their "tribulations" here is what we will find:

- They were lied upon

- Others turned against them
- They were stripped of their clothes and possessions
- They were beaten severely
- They were cast into the inner prison
- Their feet were put in stocks
- When the prison door was closed, they found themselves in darkness, and the stench of human waste
- Being in the "inner prison" they were isolated from everyone who cared about them

A note about the beatings and prison: The Romans had several devices used in beating or flogging their prisoners. A "flagrum" was used in the beating of Jesus. It was a whip with a short handle with several thick leather strips at the end of the handle. Lead weights and pieces of bone were tied to the end of each strip.   The leather strips cut the skin, and bone and weights created deep lacerations and contusions. Sometimes flesh was literally torn from the back side of prisoners exposing veins, arteries, muscles and bones. Other Roman instruments used in beatings were elm rods, wooden canes, and a variety of other whips. We are not told what device was used on Paul and Silas, but we are told that the beating was severe. Most times two or more soldiers were used to beat each prisoner. These soldiers were called *lictors*, thus the phase, "take a licking".

We are also told that they were cast into the "inner prison". Roman prisons were divided into three areas. The first area was the barracks, for prisoners who were more or less "confined to quarters" for light offenses. The next level had cells that were locked but open to light and fresh air. The "inner prison" was the worst of all. It was a room with only one entrance through the roof of the enclosure. There was little or no light, no fresh air, no running water – just darkness, and the stench of human waste.

Paul and Silas had their feet put in stocks. Roman stocks were designed not to just to make prisoners immobile, but to cause pain. There were up to five holes in some stocks and many prisoners suffered from dislocated limbs while being placed in them. So if you read the scriptures too quickly, you'll miss the real "meat" of what they endured. Paul and Silas were stripped, brutalized, and imprisoned in the worst conditions.

Although most of us will never physically experience anything as brutal as Paul and Silas' treatment, we can become emotionally stripped, brutalized and imprisoned. Because we live in an ungodly, decaying world that does not honor or know God, bad things happen. Sometimes bad things happen because of our own decisions or those made by someone close to us. Sometimes Satan tries to discourage us to keep God from receiving glory through our lives. Sometimes we can find no reason for the troubles of life; life just happens. Whatever the reason, there are times when you feel whipped and forsaken.

> *Have you or someone close to you been emotionally stripped, brutalized or imprisoned? What was your/their outlook on life? How did you/they feel about God? Have you ever felt abandoned, but yet were not physically alone? Why do does it seem like God is so far away at those times, when He's not?*

A Choice, Not A Feeling

Read Acts 16:25 – 28. This passage caught my attention and started me thinking. When I read verse 25 my first reaction was, "How in the world could they be praying and singing to God? He was the One Who allowed this to happen. They were preaching the Gospel when all this began. I don't get it."

Then I read verse 26. This was powerful; their prayer and praise to God, in the midst of their tribulation, brought them deliverance. I thought about this and wondered, "How can this be?" I was amazed by the fact that these men *chose* to sing songs of *praise* to God. It had to be more than a feeling because they had been severely beaten and were in a dark, stench filled prison; the pain of their wounds was still fresh. How can you praise God in the midst of pain? It had to be a choice, and not a feeling.

The more important question is, "How can this apply to your life, right now given your current situation? How can you make this real?" Let's look at the picture on the right and break it down step by step.

When you accepted Christ as your Savior, and believed in Him in your heart, you received His Spirit, the Holy Spirit. Read I Corinthians 3:16 – 17 and John 14:16. From these scriptures we can see that the Holy Spirit dwells in you forever. The Holy Spirit lays the foundation that enables your faith to grow.

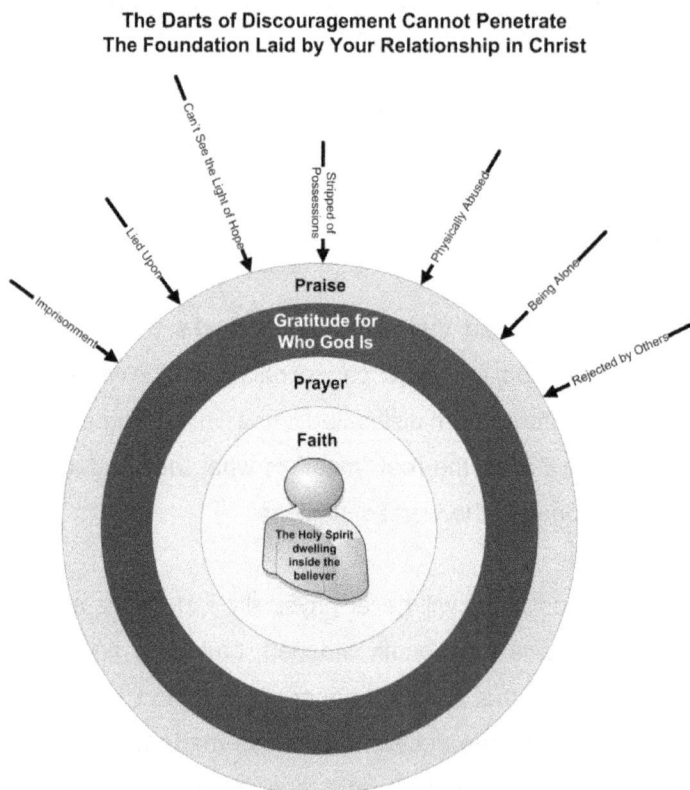

**The Darts of Discouragement Cannot Penetrate
The Foundation Laid by Your Relationship in Christ**

Imprisonment · Lied Upon · Can't See the Light of Hope · Stripped of Possessions · Physically Abused · Being Alone · Rejected by Others

Praise

Gratitude for Who God Is

Prayer

Faith

The Holy Spirit dwelling inside the believer

As you develop a *regular routine* of prayer and Bible study, your relationship and understanding of the Lord and His ways grow. Jesus told his disciples that the Holy Spirit would guide them to all truth (John 16:13). So it is with us…He guides us to the truth about Who our Father is…step by step by step; it's a process.

The Holy Spirit dwelling inside the believer

As we grow in relationship with God, our faith grows. Faith, from the Greek word "pistis", is that strong conviction as to the truth about God, His ways and character. If you keep a notebook and write down what God does for you, over time you will have documented God actively working in your life. His actions will *confirm* what the Holy Spirit reveals to you about Him. We stop praying to "someone up there, somewhere" and begin to pray to Someone we can sense, feel, and know. God becomes more familiar and real to us.

As our faith grows, our prayers become powerful and effective. As confirmation, read the second half of James 5:16. The Amplified Bible states the following. I have emphasized the last half of the verse.

Confess to one another therefore your faults (your slips, your false steps, your offenses, your sins) and pray [also] for one another, that you may be healed and restored [to a spiritual tone of mind and heart]. **The earnest (heartfelt, continued) prayer of a righteous man makes tremendous power available [dynamic in its working].**

Faith

The Holy Spirit dwelling inside the believer

When we earnestly pray for others, we see God move in their lives. This encourages us that He will work on our behalf also.

As time goes on, we come to "know" Him. "Know" from the Greek word "eidon" means the following:

- to see
- to perceive with the eyes
- to perceive by any of the senses
- to perceive, notice, discern, discover
- to turn the eyes, the mind, the attention to anything

- to pay attention, observe
- to see about something
- to ascertain what must be done about it
- to inspect, examine
- to look at, behold
- to experience any state or condition
- to see i.e. have an interview with, to visit
- to know
- to know of anything
- to know, i.e. get knowledge of, understand, perceive
- to have regard for one, cherish, pay attention to (1Th. 5:12)

Normally I wouldn't list so many definitions, but they all express a dimension to our relationship with God that reflects a part of our growth. Regular prayer and study allows us to understand and perceive Him; we ascertain what must be done because of our relationship with Him; we turn our eyes, mind and attention towards Him. The more we know Him the more we want to examine and inspect truths about Him.

Over time we develop a gratitude for not only what He does for us, *but Who He is*. It's just like the relationship between a child and a loving parent; the child loves the parent for who they are. These are signs of a growing personal relationship.

Finally, we come to a point where we can praise God in the midst of a storm. Continued practice of our "routine" strengthens and "thickens" each layer. Our faith stands firm no matter what darts are fired upon us.

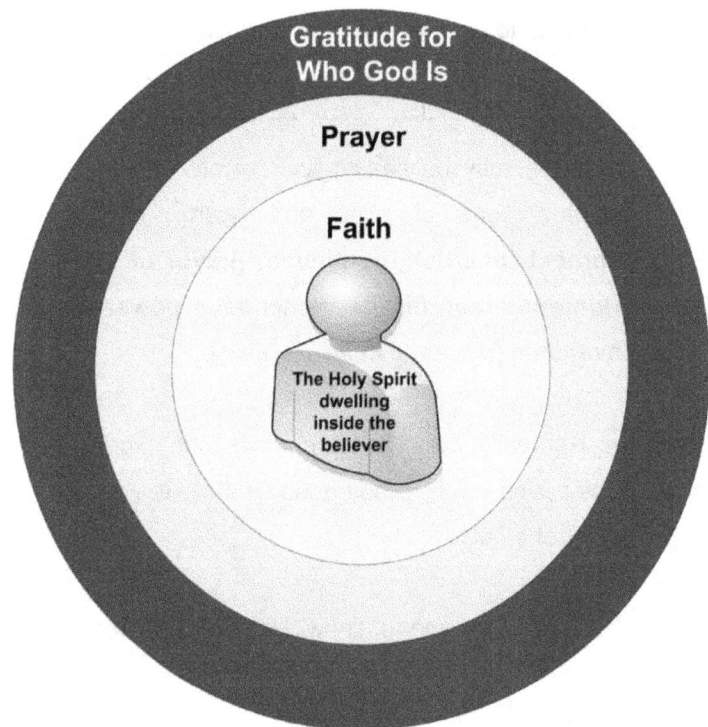

How do I know that this works? A couple in our bible study group had a son who contracted a rare disease when he was eighteen. Within months he died, never graduating from high school. Within a couple of years, the couple started a "back-to-school" celebration in their neighborhood to provide free school supplies to kids in honor of their son. Each year afterwards, kids from all over came to play games, win prizes and get free supplies. To date thousands of kids and parents have benefited from the couple's generosity.

The pain they felt at the loss of their son was real. They were emotionally stripped, brutalized and imprisoned. The emotional scars are still "tender" at times. *But the foundation of their faith allowed them to turn their grief into generosity towards others.* The most tragic "dart of discouragement" that a parent can imagine was fired at this couple, and they were not defeated. *God can and is willing to do the same for you.*

This is how He receives glory. Most parents who come to the "back-to-school" celebration don't know the story behind the couple's son; they just receive the benefits of what God can do in the lives of those who "sang songs of praise" in the "inner prison". Read 2 Corinthians 1:3 – 4. This couple lived this verse. Out of their tragedy, they were able to bring joy to others. This is in addition to the obvious comfort they could bring to other parents who have lost children.

Key Point: The *daily* building of your relationship with Christ builds the foundations that enable you to overcome *any* tribulation that comes your way.

Key Point: It's not really *you* who overcomes tribulations, but the *Christ in you*. As your relationship with Him grows, you learn to depend more and more on His abilities and not your own.

> *Do you know of someone who overcame a great trial? How did they do it? How did their relationship with God change before, during and after the trial? Do you think you could be victorious through the same trial? Why or Why not?*

If you read Acts 16:29 – 34, you can read the rest of the story and see how Paul's jailer was saved. But the key question at this time is, "What about you? How can you sing a song of praise and victory based on how you *feel* now?"

Well, based on now you *feel* now, you can't. You must *choose* to praise. Remember, it's a choice not a feeling. Also, remember that your foundations grow as your relationship with the Lord grows. So do the following:

1. Make time each day to read one chapter out of the Bible.
2. Ask the Lord to give you understanding about Him and His ways before you read.
3. Write down each week something the Lord has done positive in your life.

4. Ask the Lord to show you how to help someone else with what He's given you - your time, talents, heartaches and victories in accordance with 2 Corinthians 1:3 – 4.

5. After one month review the list.

6. Repeat steps 1 – 5.

Summary

Life is full of challenges. Life is not fair. Many things you can't control. Neither can you turn back the hands of time. You are where you are. So the most important question to ask is, "Where do I go from here?" The answer is, "Closer to the Lord." He is the only resource you have to overcome your challenge(s). Sympathy, well wishes, and good intentions are nice, but don't give you victory – only a growing *personal* relationship with Christ gives you victory. Make a decision today to *choose* Christ; make a decision today to "sing".

Notes:

Why We Fall Short - Part 1

Introduction

Recently I asked the Lord, "Lord, why are Your children falling short of all that You have provided for them in this world." My question stemmed from the realization that most Christians never experience the "abundance" that God has provided for us. We don't experience the peace, joy, and security that are available to us through God's Word. The Bible is full of promises for the Christian that we don't fully experience. As I reflected on my own life, I wondered, "Why?"

The answer I got was short and to the point, "Sin." I was expecting a different answer with several "reasons". But this is what I got, short and to the point. So I thought about His answer.

This study is designed to help fellow Christians see possible shortcomings of their lives that prevent them from experiencing the "abundance" God has graciously provided for His children to lead victorious lives through any trial.

Scriptures Used in This Lesson

Romans 12:1 – 2
Leviticus 27:30
Acts 4:32 – 37
Ephesians 4:14 – 15
Proverbs 3:5 – 6
Romans 8:28 – 30
Proverbs 6:16 – 19
Genesis 3:1 – 7

A Word About Sin and Relationships

Most of the time when we think of sin, we think of it as something bad that we've done, like lying, stealing, cheating, committing a murder...the "big" sins. God wants us to see that there a "little" things, or sometimes "subtle" things that we do that are contrary to His character.

First, let's define sin. In the Old Testament, "sin" comes from the word "chata" which means:

- to sin, miss, miss the way, go wrong, incur guilt, forfeit

A corresponding word from the New Testament is "hamartano" which means:

- to be without a share in

- to miss the mark
- to err, be mistaken
- to miss or wander from the path of uprightness and honor, to do or go wrong
- to wander from the law of God, violate God's law, sin

There are several other words used for "sin" in the Bible, but I want to define it in terms of God's character and our personal relationship to Him. *When we "sin", we "miss the mark", i.e., we do, say, and think things that are contrary to His character and are damaging to our personal relationship with Him.* When we think of God's character as being "perfect", then this opens the door to many things that can separate us from Him. So anything that separates us from Him is "sin".

A word about personal relationships: When we think of having a personal relationship with someone, we usually imply that we have something in common with the other person. We may have the same interests, political views, favorite sports team, or vocation. If we describe the relationship as being a "close" personal relationship, we imply that there is a common bond between us that goes beyond intellectual commonalities. We know each other at a deeper level. Sometimes we can communicate with each other without words.

For example, we refer to a basketball team as being "close" where the players know each other's abilities and tendencies so well that they can anticipate their teammates' moves before they make them. The team is able to run plays smoothly and effectively. This type of closeness requires many hours of practicing together.

In a marriage, a husband and wife become "close" by spending time with each other. Each knows how the other will respond to things before they happen. One spouse can "read" the other spouse by the way they look or move, in subtle ways that most people would miss. As they become closer, each spouse may even take on some behaviors of the other spouse.

In our relationship with the Lord, "closeness" comes with spending time with Him. We get to know Him so well that He can communicate with us "without spoken words". In fact, He does this through the Holy Spirit. When we are close to God, we know what pleases and displeases Him. In this sense, we can "anticipate" His "reaction". In addition, as we get closer to the Lord, we tend to take on His character traits. We are "transformed by the renewing of our minds". Read Romans 12:1 – 2.

So sin is anything that damages that transformation process; that makes us less like God in our thinking, character, and actions. Sin exposes our corrupt human nature instead of the nature of our

Savior. It destroys the closeness between us and Him, and prevents us from fulfilling His will for our lives.

The Subtle Sins

Below we'll address several areas of "sin" which are more subtle than the "big sins" (lying, cheating, and stealing), but are just as detrimental to our personal relationship with the Lord.

Tithes and Offerings

There has been controversy over this subject for years, but I've grown to understand how important tithing is in the believer's life.

Read Leviticus 27:30. God considers the tithe as "holy". "Holy" comes from the word "qodesh" which means "set apart or sacred". God lays claim to His portion of our increase. Why is that? It's not like God "needs" money or fruits or vegetables. Well, it all goes back to relationship.

When we tithe, we are acknowledging that God is the source of our income. It is an expression of our relationship showing our trust in Him, our acknowledgement of Him being the source of our increase, and our thankfulness. It also financially supports the activities which have a positive impact in the lives of those in the church and in the community.

When we tithe, we are in effect saying:

> "Lord, I am giving You 10% of my income and I am trusting You to provide for all the needs I have that this 10% could meet. I am actually trusting that You will meet more needs than this 10% represents. I am trusting You to be faithful in Your care for me."

Key Point: The tithe is a reflection of our relationship with God. It's a matter of trust and obedience.

Why do people hold on to money so dearly? Why don't we, as Christians, acknowledge that God owns it all? What can help Christians see things differently?

Concerning thanksgiving: First of all, God does not need money. He already owns it all and the means to create it. There is nothing good that we own that did not come from God either directly or indirectly. There is no set of skills or aptitudes that we possess that did not come from God. As creator of all things, *God owns it all*. There are no "self-made men"; only men who have been endowed by God with certain gifts, talents and opportunities.

When we tithe, we are expressing thanks to Him for what He has done in our lives; for His blessings. We could not even live without Him. So the fact that He blesses us with increase is "icing on the cake" so to speak.

By tithing to an organization that's positively impacting lives of people, we are extending the reach of God's love. Acts 4:32 – 37 is an ideal example of how giving can and should affect the lives of others.

To "not tithe" shows distrust; it places the honor of being the source of our increase on someone or something else, and it shows ungratefulness. It's really an insult to God. It's like a teenager going across town to a person they don't know and thanking them for all that their parents provide – food, clothing, a car to drive and car insurance, housing, spending money, etc.

Key Point: God owns it all.

<u>Manipulation</u>

One of the most subtle sins is manipulation. It's part of our fallen, human nature. Children exhibit manipulative skills at an early age. Don't think so? Well picture this:

A little girl crawls up into her daddy's lap and cuddles up to him. This man, who was intently watching television, all of a sudden breaks out in a big smile, and wraps his arms around his daughter and says, "Hey Sweetie. You come to see Daddy?" The little girls says in the sweetest tone, "Daddy", and she pauses to make sure she has his attention. Then, while she plays with the buttons on his shirt, she asks, "Daddy, can you buy me a dolly tomorrow?" He then smiles and says, "Why sure Sweetie. You can have anything you want." She immediately says, "Thank you Daddy." Then like, "Mission accomplished!", she jumps down and goes back to her room to continue playing with the dolls she currently owns.

This scene is very familiar to all of us. We have either seen it played out or may have been one of the actors in the scene. The child learned, at an early age, how to approach her father to get what she wants. She didn't go see her father to check on his welfare or to keep him company; she wanted something for herself and used the skills that came "natural" to her to get what she wanted, a new doll.

By definition, manipulation is:

to control or play upon by artful, unfair, or <u>insidious</u> means especially to one's own advantage

The above scene with the little girl and her father seems innocent enough, but as we get older, our "artful means" become more sophisticated. The goal is the same – to get what we want – but the techniques become more subtle. We've all seen situations where one person exhibits an unusually strong influence over another that is detrimental to the person who is being controlled. Or a scene where one worker "plays up to the boss" to improve his/her chances for advancement. Or a salesperson who smiles and becomes your "instant" friend until the purchase is final.

Sin, in general, works in the same way. The definition of "insidious" bears mention:

> **1 a** : *awaiting a chance to entrap : treacherous* **b** : *harmful but enticing : seductive <insidious drugs>*
> **2 a** : *having a gradual and cumulative effect : subtle <the insidious pressures of modern life>* **b** *of a disease :* **developing so gradually as to be well established before becoming apparent**

In our "little girl" story, her influence over the father developed so gradually that it was well established before she knew what she was doing and before he caught on. The desire was "minor", a doll, but the *process* was the same as that used by adults. Sin in our lives (either being the manipulator or the one manipulated) usually comes gradually. We usually don't see its effect until it's too late. And its effects can be cumulative.

The Bible uses the word "craftiness". Read Ephesians 4:14 – 15 below from the NIV:

> Then we will no longer be infants, tossed back and forth by the waves, and blown here and there by every wind of teaching and by the cunning and *craftiness* of men in their deceitful scheming. Instead, speaking the truth in love, we will in all things grow up into him who is the Head, that is, Christ.

The word "craftiness" comes from the Greek word "panourgia" which means having a deceptive attraction or false wisdom.

> *Can manipulation be "good"? If you think that sometimes it's for someone else's welfare, do you think the end justifies the means? Is it okay to be deceptive if you*

judge the end to be "good"? Do you think this behavior is in keeping with the character of God?

Key Point: Any behavior in which we engage that is contrary to the character of God, leads us away from Him. Therefore it is sin.

The diagram below shows graphically how manipulation works.

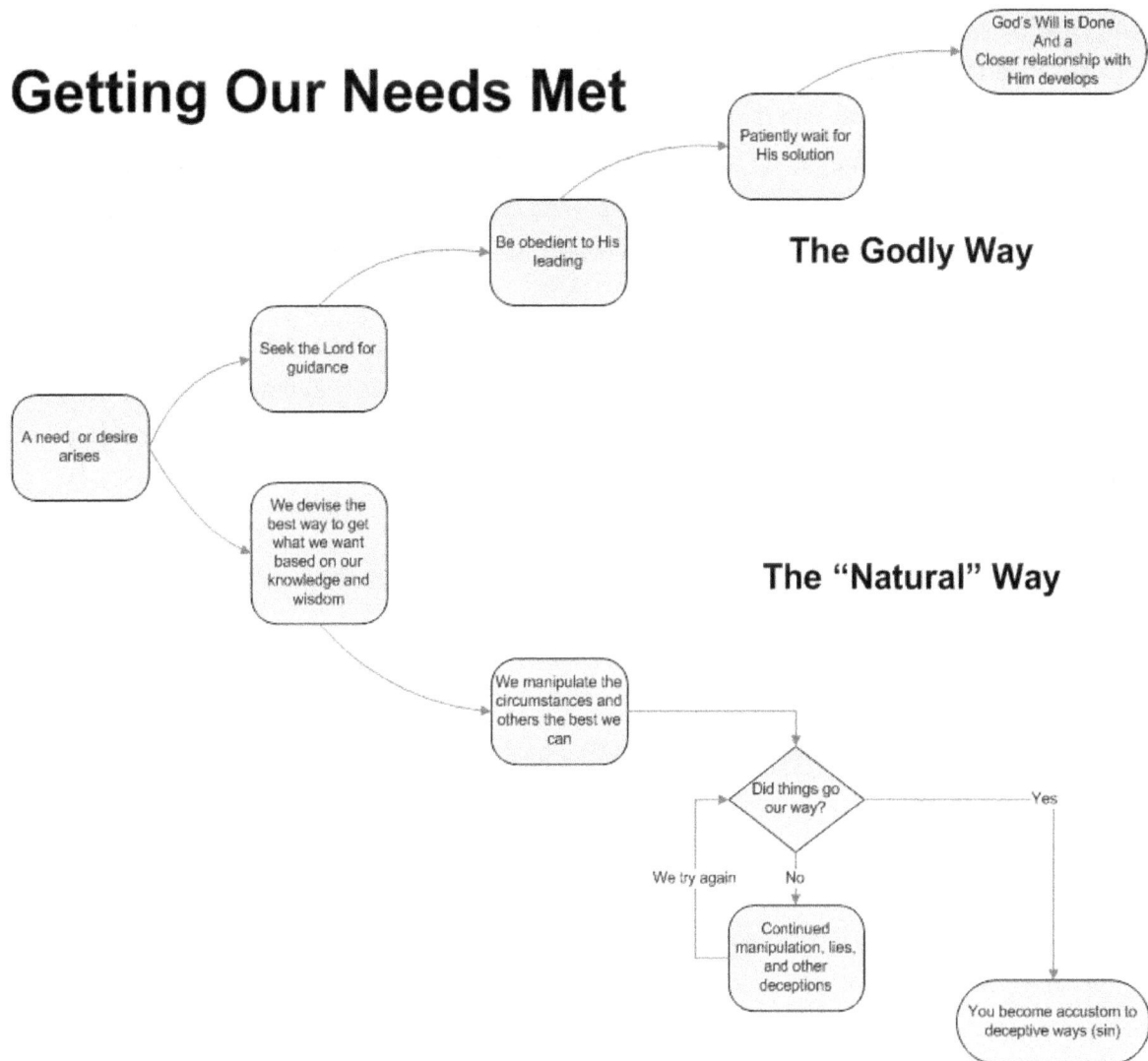

Getting Our Needs Met

A need or desire arises

Seek the Lord for guidance

Be obedient to His leading

Patiently wait for His solution

God's Will is Done And a Closer relationship with Him develops

The Godly Way

We devise the best way to get what we want based on our knowledge and wisdom

The "Natural" Way

We manipulate the circumstances and others the best we can

Did things go our way?

Yes

We try again   No

Continued manipulation, lies, and other deceptions

You become accustom to deceptive ways (sin)

When a need first arises, "naturally" we devise our own ways of getting our needs met. Unfortunately we do not consult the Lord; we act in ignorance, i.e., we rarely know all the facts of a situation. Next we begin to manipulate our circumstances and people around us to get what we want. Our "panourgia" leads us into deception. If we get what we want, then we are more inclined to repeat our actions. Over time we grow accustom to deceptive ways and those ways can permeate into other areas of our lives.

If we don't get our way, we try, again, and again, until we get the results we want. The driving force behind our actions becomes *getting what we want*. On the surface, this may appear to be "good" for us or someone else, but leaves God out of the picture, who knows all of the facts of the situation including the future.

This "way" is in direct conflict with the instructions given to us in Proverbs 3:5 – 6. It actually makes logical sense to trust God. For example, who would you prefer to perform brain surgery on you, a skilled surgeon who has studied for ten years and has another fifteen years of experience, or a high school student who saw a program about brains on the *Discovery Channel*®? The obvious answer is the experienced surgeon. Then who is best at solving our problems, the One who knows everything and has experience with every situation we will ever come across, or ourselves?

Notice that the end result of the "godly" way is not necessarily what we want, but God's will. Since God has all the facts and has a perfect plan for our lives, He will work out the situation for our good. Read Romans 8:28 – 30. If the one we are trying to manipulate has accepted Christ, then God will work things out for their good. We have to trust Him.

Key Point: The root of manipulation is selfishness.

Key Point: The means by which manipulation is carried out is deception.

Read Proverbs 6:16 – 19. These are the things God hates. Manipulation:

- Can be driven by pride
- Is carried out by deception
- Involves a victim, and can adversely affect the innocent
- Involves devising schemes which are contrary to the character of God
- Is mischievous, tends to cause annoyance, trouble, or minor injury
- Can involve lies
- Can be used to sow discord

Key Point: You can't justify sin to obtain a "good" goal. Put another way, the end does not justify the means when it comes to maintaining a pure heart before the Lord.

Do you agree with the key point above? Why or why not?

How can we live without manipulation? By trusting and obeying God. God loves the people we love more than we do. God knows what is best for us better than we do. God can move others to work in our behalf better than any of our efforts. God knows it all, owns it all, and can do it all. We need to surrender our desires and situations to God. We need to seek His guidance to see what is our role (if any), and then leave the consequences to Him.

When we see God working on our behalf, we are always amazed at His works. This "amazement" excites us and drives us to trust Him more. This leads to a closer relationship with Him, which is His ultimate goal.

Rationalization

Rationalization is another "subtle sin" in which we engage, sometimes on a daily basis. Children exhibit this ability at an early age. To rationalize means to:

- cause something to seem reasonable
- to create an excuse or more attractive explanation for
- to provide plausible but untrue reasons for conduct

We've all seen a situation where a child was caught doing something they shouldn't have been doing. When asked, "Why did you do that?", they provide an "excuse" that makes it seem "okay". Rationalization goes on every day. Here are some examples:

1. A child "sneaks" a cookie out of the kitchen before dinner. He/she decides that since they were going to get it any way, they might as well get it now.

2. A high school student moves out of the house to live with her boy friend in an apartment. They are planning to get married anyway, so they might as well live together now.

3. A college student cheats on an exam. "Everyone else is doing it".

4. A business man "adjusts" the financial books of a company to make them look good for the quarterly review. He didn't do anything "illegal", but the financial report really does not reflect the "true" quarterly performance. If you make your boss look good, then you have a better chance at being promoted.

5. A man stays at home on Sunday and decides to let his wife and children go to church while he catches the early football games on television. As long as the rest of the family is getting something spiritual, everything is okay.

6. A young man decides not to pray. His grandmother is praying for him.

7. Over 50% of black babies are born to single parent homes. The white man has created an environment that keeps blacks in a cycle of poverty, hopelessness, and despair.

8. A congressman sends sexually explicit e-mails to a minor. He claims he was abused by a priest 30 years prior to his encounter with the minor.

9. I walked out and left my wife and kids. I need to find *my* happiness.

10. I can't speak out against homosexual activity among members of my congregation. The couples look so happy together. The Bible is kind of "fuzzy" anyway.

11. I cheated on my taxes, but the government wastes all that money anyway.

12. I don't read my Bible on a daily basis. I go to church on occasions. God knows my heart.

13. We need to pass the stem cell initiative in our state and protect that research by amending the constitution. We need to make sure that any future treatments are available to us.

When is rationalization good? Are any of the "rationales" provided above legitimate? Why or why not? Which one have you or someone you know used recently?

The Process of Rationalization

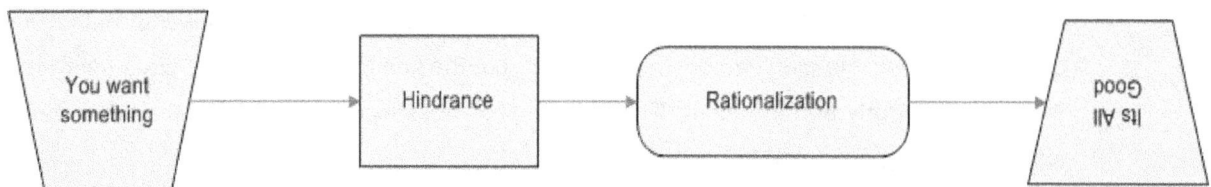

The process of rationalization starts with a desire – you want something or you want to do something. The action may or may not be "wrong"; it might be a case where we want something now and don't want to wait for it.

The next step involves a hindrance to your having what you want. Then the process of rationalization occurs. We find reasons to justify our actions, i.e., explain why we did what we did so that it appears "acceptable" to ourselves and others. In effect we turn things upside down.

The first encounter of rationalization occurred in the Garden of Eden. Read Genesis 3:1 – 7. First of all Eve was deceived in verse 4. After eating the fruit, both Adam and Eve were spiritually separated from God. The key verse is verse 6. She saw the fruit was "good for food, pleasing to the eye, and desirable for gaining wisdom". She focused on all the "positives" of the fruit, and turned the fruit from something to be avoided to something to possess; from something bad to something good.

It is not uncommon for rationalization to involve some sort of deception, i.e., to cause to accept as true or valid what is false or invalid. This deception makes engaging in the act more acceptable. Many times we will even deceive ourselves. Emotionally we'll focus on the rationalization (which makes our action positive) instead of the "truth" (which makes our actions negative).

Now, why is rationalization bad? Too often it is used to cover up our sins; to explain away our disobedience and flaws. It puts our desires first above what is right, legal, appropriate, or best. It is a process by which we put our desires above God's. It is contrary to the character of God. God has never been "wishy-washy" about anything. He is straight forward and clear. The Ten Commandments weren't given as suggestions. And anything that is contrary to the character, ways and laws of God, inhibits our personal relationship with Him. Those ways lead us to sin.

The Rationalization List

Review the list of common "rationalization starting points" and see which one(s) apply to you:

1. I didn't study my bible because…
2. I didn't witness because…
3. I'm late because…
4. I didn't keep my word because…
5. I ate too much because…
6. I didn't listen to your advice because…
7. I'm bitter because…
8. I didn't tithe because…

9. I cheated on my spouse because…

10. I look at pornography, because…

11. I lied because…

12. I cheated because…

13. I stole because…

14. I quit my job because…

15. I cussed out my boss/co-worker because…

16. I got drunk because…

17. I killed that person in my thoughts because…

18. I hate my father/mother/sister/brother/relative because…

19. I failed in business/a job/a task because…

20. I didn't pay my bills because…

21. I manipulate because…

22. I don't trust God because…

23. I'm disobedient to God because…

The key is that we must put our personal relationship with the Lord above everything else. Nothing else in our lives will be "right" until we get that relationship "right".

Key Point: Any thing, or process in which we engage, that damages our relationship with the Lord is not good.

Summary

God has made available a multitude of blessings for each one of His children that are the result of a personal relationship with Him. But yet we routinely fall short of realizing these blessing in our lives because of "subtle sins". Some sin comes so "natural" to us that we don't even view it as sin. The affects are the same, missed blessings of health, prosperity, hope, joy, and peace of mind. Hopefully this lesson will cause you to look at yourselves honestly and critically so you can make the changes necessary to get closer to your Heavenly Father.

Notes:

Why We Fall Short - Part 2

Introduction

Part 1 of this lesson started with my asking the Lord, "Why are Your children falling short of all You have provided for them in this world." His answer was short and to the point, "Sin." Because of our fallen nature, we have tendencies to engage in some areas of sin so "naturally" that we don't even see it as sin. But the effects on our relationship with the Lord are the same as if we routinely engaged in bank robberies.

Part 1 of this study dealt with tithing, manipulation and rationalization. This study focuses on unfaithfulness, lack of love, and no acknowledgement of God as presented in the book of Hosea. The goal for us is to recognize these subtle areas of sin in our lives and to be restored to a right relationship with our Heavenly Father.

Scriptures Used in This Lesson

Hosea 4:1 – 3

Galatians 5:22 – 23

James 5:16

Hosea 8:11 – 14

John 8:30

Colossians 1:18 – 20

Hebrews 1:3

Ephesians 5:1 – 2

I Peter 1:14 – 16

Colossians 3:17

Colossians 3:1 – 17

Hosea 8:1 – 4

Hosea 13:2

Hosea 12:8

Exodus 20: 3 – 4

Hosea 13:6

Psalm 103:1

Background on Hosea

Hosea was a prophet of God who lived in Israel during a chaotic period where the nation had six kings in about 25 years. During this time, Israel was invaded by the Assyrians in 733 BC and finally conquered in 722 BC. We don't know much about Hosea's life outside of this book, but we do know that he lived during the mid-700's BC. Hosea, whose name means "salvation", prophesized about

Israel's sin and encouraged them to repent and restore a right relationship with the Lord. If they had listened, they would have received "salvation"; unfortunately they did not.

What is unusual about his ministry is that God told Hosea to marry a prostitute named Gomer. His relationship with his wife was symbolic of the relationship between God and Israel. Gomer was unfaithful to Homer; Israel was unfaithful to God. Hosea and Gomer had three children, Jezreel which means "God scatters", Lo-Ruhamah which means "not loved", and Lo-Ammi which means "not my people". The names of his children are indicative of Israel's condition because of her sin before the Lord. Spiritually speaking, they were the off-spring of someone who was unfaithful. After nearly four decades of ignoring the warnings of Hosea, Israel finally fell to the Assyrians and was "driven to her knees".

Where We Fall Short

Now how does this relate to us? Israel committed many sins, but there were three main categories under which their sin fell. Read Hosea 4:1 – 3. Verse 1 outlines the categories:

The King James Version (KJV) lists the categories as:

- No truth
- No mercy
- No knowledge of God in the land

The New International Version (NIV) translates the categories as:

- Unfaithfulness
- Lack of love
- No acknowledgement of God in the land.

We'll look at the Hebrew words for each one of these and see that the translations are not dissimilar.

Unfaithfulness

In Hosea 4:1, the KJV lists a lack of "truth" to be the first category of sin. The Hebrew word is "'emeth", which means:

        1) firmness, *faithfulness*, truth
            a) sureness, reliability
            b) stability, continuance

c) *faithfulness, reliableness*

d) truth

- as spoken
- of testimony and judgment
- of divine instruction
- truth as a body of ethical or religious knowledge
- true doctrine

(Emphasis is mine)

The word refers not only to "truth" as in a "true doctrine", but of "faithfulness. Faithfulness is a "fruit of the Spirit". Read Galatians 5:22 – 23. The King James Version uses the word "faith". Other translations use the word "faithfulness". In the Greek, the word is "pistis" which means:

1. *a conviction or belief respecting man's relationship to God and divine things, generally with the included idea of trust and holy fervor born of faith and joined with it*

2. the conviction that God exists and is the creator and ruler of all things, the provider and bestower of eternal salvation through Christ

3. a strong and welcome conviction or belief that Jesus is the Messiah, through whom we obtain eternal salvation in the kingdom of God

4. the religious beliefs of Christians

5. belief with the predominate idea of trust (or confidence) whether in God or in Christ, springing from faith in the same

6. *fidelity, faithfulness*

    a. *the character of one who can be relied on*

(Emphasis is mine)

In item #1 of the definition above, faithfulness is associated with "holy fervor". Fervor means intense feeling or expression. For many Christians, our "faith" is not intense; we are casual with our faith. *It's as though our faith is like an article of clothing that we put on and take off when it's convenient or necessary; clothing designed for "show". Instead, faith should be a part of us like an arm or a leg; a necessary part of our lives.*

This is particularly true of our prayer life. Read James 5:16. The King James Version uses the words "effectual", "fervent", and "availeth". Using the definitions of these words and paraphrasing the second half of the verse, we get:

Prayers that are sincere, heart-felt, and intense, have power as shown by extraordinary deeds.

If our prayers are casual, i.e., not sincere, heart-felt or intense, they will be "ineffective". If our faith in Christ is casual, we can expect the similar results. This condition is unacceptable to God. He desires intimacy with His children. In order to achieve a level of intimacy, He allows us to go through difficult times to "drive us to our knees". This results is our seeking Him more intently. Our unfaithfulness is damaging to our personal relationship with our Father. As a result, we miss out on some of the benefits of that relationship.

When are your prayers the most sincere and intense? What prevents us from keeping a high level of intensity in our prayer life and our faith? What can we do to change it and be more consistent?

Key Point: God demands an increasing level of intimacy with His children. Anything less is unacceptable.

Item #6 in the above definition addresses another area in which we fall short. A person who exhibits "faithfulness" can be described as:

- Reliable
- Loyal
- Steadfast (immovable)
- Consistent
- Resolute (firm determination)

We usually exhibit faithfulness in only certain areas of our lives — seeking entertainment, eating, the praise of other people — those areas which gratify us (or more precisely, our flesh). But are we faithful in the areas that matter most: our families, the call of God on our lives, using our talents and skills to honor Him and build the ministry?

How reliable are you in the things of God? Which do you pursue with more fervor, a meal, or time with God? Can others who are trying to build a ministry rely on you? If not, why? What legacy do you want to build while you have the opportunity?

No relationship can grow, have meaning, or be effective without faithfulness, "pistis", "holy fervor", resolve or determination. Inconsistency, disloyalty, hypocrisy, and being unreliable in the things of God are what angered God in the book of Hosea. Read Hosea 8:11 – 14.

As stated in the definition above, faithfulness is the "character of one who can be relied on". Can God rely on you?

Key Point: Faithfulness (being reliable and consistent) is necessary for any relationship to prosper.

How does faithfulness (or the lack thereof) affect a business relationship? How does faithfulness (or the lack thereof) affect a personal relationship? Our spiritual relationship with God? How does it affect the purpose of God in our lives?

Lack of Love

Back in Hosea 4:1, the Lord says that there was a "lack of love". The King James Version translation says there was "no mercy". The Hebrew word is "chesed", which means:

- Kindness, good deed, favor
- With respect towards God, piety

So the Bible states that there was a lack of kindness, good deeds and showing respectful devotion towards God. This is illustrated in Hosea 4:2.

The KJV states:

By swearing, and lying, and killing, and stealing, and committing adultery, they break out, and blood toucheth blood.

The same verse in the NIV reads:

There is only cursing, lying and murder, stealing and adultery; they break all bounds, and bloodshed follows bloodshed.

The Amplified Bible reads:

There is nothing but [false] swearing and breaking faith and killing and stealing and committing adultery; they break out [into violence], one [deed of] bloodshed following close on another.

The lack of love is obvious. So how does this relate to us?

We may not commit murder, but subtleties in other sins are more common.

- When was the last time you told a "white lie"? Do you find yourself telling one lie to cover up another lie, to cover up another?
- When was the last time you intentionally deceived or manipulated someone?
- When was the last time you refused to show forgiveness or kindness to someone?
- When was the last time you let yourself get too busy, and when it came to helping someone, you "just didn't get around to it"?
- Do you have gifts, talents, and skills that can help others that are not being put to use?
- Do you find yourself being self-centered and concerned only with getting your needs and desires met?
- Is the only time you give to others is on birthdays and Christmas?
- Do you give to others with the expectation or hope of getting something back in return?

When God shows us favor, it is undeserved. But when He does, it lifts our spirits and always comes "right on time". God is looking for us to be an extension of His nature and character. Jesus is an exact representation of God and we are to imitate Christ in our daily walk. Read John 10:30, Colossians 1:18 – 20, Hebrews 1:3, Ephesians 5:1 – 2, I Peter 1:14 – 16.

Christ is the exact representation of God. And we are to be representatives of Christ. Colossians 3:17 instructs us to do all things "in the name of the Lord Jesus", i.e., in a manner, attitude, and character that is representative of Christ. When we look at Christ, He showed compassion in addressing people's spiritual, emotional and physical needs. He demonstrated the Love of the Father. He demonstrated kindness. We are to do the same. Read Colossians 3:1 – 17. These are rules for holy living.

Key Point: When God gives to us, it is out of love. We are to do the same. (Colossians 3:12 – 13)

Key Point: Love is more than a feeling; it is also a choice.

Lack of Acknowledgement of God

The "lack of acknowledgement of God" in Hosea 4:1, goes beyond verbal, superficial statements that include His name. The "acknowledgement" is indicative of relationship. Read Hosea 8:1 – 4.

Verse 4 is particularly pertinent. Israel had "set up kings", but not by the Lord. They had selected princes, but again, not by the Lord. They made idols with the silver and gold. Hosea 13:2 provides an example where the people would "kiss" their idols. These examples show how their hearts and minds were far from God.

Read Hosea 12:8. Here we see a case where the people were thinking that because of their "riches", they were without sin. Israel was truly far from God. Their personal relationship with Him had diminished to the extent that they did not think about Him, nor consult Him when they were making significant decisions. They did not give him credit for what He had done in their lives. They did not give Him thanks. They were superficial in their mention of Him; "their hearts were not in it". They even did the things which were explicitly and strictly forbidden in the Ten Commandments (Exodus 20:3 – 4).

How does this relate to us, today, in our modern world, even though we are Christians? First of all:

- How often do you think about the Lord during the day? Are you conscious of Him throughout the day, or do you just think about Him as an afterthought at night before you pray? Or do you even pray at all, except on Sunday's when the pastor/priest prays?

- Do you say the same prayers, in the same way over and over again, with no real thought to the words?

- Do you consider yourself a "good" person? Have you ever meditated on your nature compared to that of Christ's?

- Do you only pray when things go bad?

- Do you ever ask the Lord for direction when faced with a decision? How often and under what conditions?

- When you pray do you only "ask for stuff", as a little child would do with their parent?

- How often do you give the Lord thanks, from the heart?

- When things are going well for you, how intently do you pray or do you pray at all? Does Hosea 13:6 describe your relationship with the Lord when things go well for you?

These are areas where we often fall short in our relationship with God. Christ is supposed to be the center of our lives, not our spouses, kids, jobs, trials and tribulations – just Christ. When we remove Him from the center, our lives get out of balance and we tend to not acknowledge Him. Our relationship with Him suffers. As a result, we miss out on blessings that He has provided for us.

"Fervor" or "passion" should describe our relationship to the Lord. Read Psalm 103:1.

The Amplified Bible reads:

> BLESS (AFFECTIONATELY, gratefully praise) the Lord, O my soul; and all that is [deepest] within me, bless His holy name!

The verse reads "all that is deepest within me". If we gratefully praise the Lord with "passion", then we will acknowledge Him throughout the day. If He is our life, then our thoughts will be towards Him. Acknowledgement of the Lord will come naturally.

> *What's at the center of your life? When was the last time you prayed with "all that was deepest within" you? If Christ is not at the center of your life, why not? What's holding you back?*

Summary

God has provided a number of blessings for each one of His children. But yet we routinely fall short of realizing these blessings because of "subtle sins". Some sin comes so "natural" to us that we don't even view it as sin. But, the affects are the same – missed blessings of peace, prosperity, hope, joy, and peace of mind. Hopefully this lesson will cause you to look at yourself honestly and critically so you can make the changes necessary to get closer to your Heavenly Father, through Christ, by the power of the Holy Spirit.

Notes:

Jesus, Where Were You When I Needed You?

Introduction

In the life of a Christian there will come times when a crisis occurs and we look to God for help, but we don't see Him. We know He has said that He will never leave us nor forsake us, but we don't see Him intervening like we want. Over time, our worst fears are realized and we are left to deal with the aftermath of the crisis. We wonder, "Where was Jesus? If He had been there, I would not have suffered."

These are the questions that faced two sisters in the book of John. This lesson is designed to help us understand, on a deeper level, the faithfulness of God and His love for us, regardless of the circumstances.

Scriptures Used In This Lesson

John 11:1 – 45

James 5:16

John 3:16

I Peter 5:6 – 7

Isaiah 55:8 – 11

Background

Jesus had just left Jerusalem where He had encountered some Jews that were trying to stone Him for His claim to be God. (John 10:22 – 42). He stayed at a place near the location where John the Baptist had baptized his followers. That's where He received word that His friend Lazarus was sick.

Jesus had become close friends with Lazarus and his two sisters, Mary and Martha. They lived in the town of Bethany which was about a day's journey (on foot) from where Jesus was staying. This study will focus mainly on John 11:1 – 45.

What's He Doin'?

Read John 11:1 – 3. This provides additional background for the study. Note that in verse 3, Jesus receives word from Mary and Martha that "the friend that He loves is sick". The word "love" (or loveth in the King James Version) is from the Greek word "phileo", which indicates "brotherly love". This supports the fact that Jesus was close friends with Lazarus and his sisters. Also note that when Lazarus became sick, they called on Jesus for help.

This scene is similar to our lives as Christians. We have established a relationship with Christ by accepting Him as our Savior. Hopefully we have made an effort to build our relationship with Him through prayer and the study of God's Word. When we come face-to-face with an obstacle, our first response should be to call upon the Lord. If it's not the first thing we do, it should be a close second.

In the case of Mary and Martha, they were faced with a situation that was totally beyond their control, i.e., the illness of their brother. They did the right thing – they called for Jesus.

> *How close is your relationship with Jesus? The last time a crisis occurred, how long did it take for you to seek the Lord? What was the first thing you did? The second? If it wasn't the first thing you did, why did it take you so long to seek the Lord? What got in your way?*

> *How did you respond to challenges when you were a "young Christian"? How do you respond to challenges now? Is there much difference? Why or Why not?*

Now read verses 4 – 6. First of all the word "love" in verse 5 is "agapeo" which is used to describe the "God-kind-of-love"; the highest order of love that is sacrificial in nature. Mary and Martha described Jesus' love for their brother as "phileo", or brotherly love in verse 3. Verse 5 tells us that Jesus had the highest order of love for Lazarus. (This is the same word used in John 3:16).

Keep this in mind; Jesus has the same love for us – even in our darkest hour, "agapeo" still flows our way. Jesus, by agapeo, sacrificed His life so that we could have a restored relationship with God and know Him as our Heavenly Father.

Verse 6 made me wonder, "What's He doin'?". Our expectation is that when we call upon His name, based on our relationship with Him, He would come to our aid, immediately. Jesus deliberately waited two days after hearing that Lazarus was sick. This is the same Lazarus that verse 5 tells us that Jesus had "agapeo" love for. So on the surface, it looks as though Jesus' agapeo for Lazarus involved Him waiting two more days and allowing him to die.

> *Why do you think Jesus waited? Have you ever called upon the Lord and it seemed as though He didn't show up, i.e., your worst fears came to pass? Why do you think Jesus waited in your situation? How did you feel – angry, disappointed, confused?*

Read verses 7 – 16. Verses 7 – 10 have been interpreted as Jesus saying that they should take advantage of the time they had to do what was needed to be done.

By the time Jesus decides to go to Bethany, we are told, by Jesus, that Lazarus was dead. On the surface there seems to be a contradiction; in verse 4 Jesus says that "This sickness will not end in death." (NIV). But Jesus Himself informs us that Lazarus had died. For Mary and Martha, the worst had come, i.e., the death of their brother. Sometimes the same is true in our lives.

There are times when it seems like it's "too late". When we needed Jesus and called for Him, He didn't show up. Our hearts posed the question: "Jesus, where were you when I needed you?" We reached the end of our faith. What we had feared came upon us.

> *Have you ever been disappointed by God? How did you feel about Him then? How do you feel about Him now? If you came back to Him, why?*

Note verse 15. Jesus says that He was "glad" that He was not there for the disciples' sake...so they could believe. Think about it – Jesus had "agapeo" love for Lazarus, but was "glad" He was not there with Lazarus so the disciples could believe in Him. The human side says, "How can you love someone and let them die?" The spiritual side says, "Lord, I love your regardless."

The Rest Of The Story

Now there is a "rest of the story". It begins with Jesus' encounter with Martha, verses 17 – 27. Pay particular attention to verses 21 and 22.

Martha was the first to come to Jesus when He arrived in Bethany. The first words out of her mouth are similar to what we would utter, hence the title of the study, "Jesus, where were you when I needed you?" But verse 22 indicates hope.

Verse 21 shows the human side of Martha (and of ourselves). Verse 22 shows the spiritual side – the one that is still holding on to hope; the hope in the nature of Who Jesus is; the knowledge that He can do anything.

Those two verses exemplify the battle that goes on in us everyday, the flesh verses the Spirit, despair verses hope, fear verses faith. Whether or not we are able to make the transition from fear to faith depends on:

- The circumstance – people have different abilities to handle different situations, based on how we were raised and our natural tendencies. Some people have a tendency to react emotionally, while others are more stoic in their reaction.

- Our prayer life – being "prayed up" is key to *responding* appropriately to a situation as opposed to *reacting* to it. An active and fervent prayer life draws us closer to our Father. Read James 5:16. Pay close attention to the second half of the verse.

  The King James Version reads:

  …The effectual, fervent prayer of a righteous man availeth much.

  The verse contains words we don't use very much, but deserve a closer look.

  "Effectual" comes from the Greek word "energeo", from which we derive the word "energy". "Energeo" means:

  > 1) to be operative, be at work, put forth power
  > 2) to work for one, aid one
  > 3) to effect
  > 4) to display one's activity, show one's self operative

  "Fervent" comes from the Greek word "ektenes", which means without ceasing, or exhibiting great intensity of feeling.

  "Availeth" comes from the Greek word "ischou", which means to be strong, to have power, to have power as shown by extraordinary deeds.

  So when we put this all together, the understanding we should receive is this:

  > "Prayers that are effective, intense, heartfelt and without ceasing, have power that will be shown by extraordinary deeds."

  > *How intense are your prayers? Under what conditions do they become "fervent"?*

  A fervent, effectual prayer life will empower us to operate in faith instead of fear.

- How much Word is in us – If you're in a battle with a gun and no bullets, you won't be able to fight off the enemy very long. You need ammunition to fight effectively. The Word of God is our ammunition for life. The more we have in us, i.e., the better we know God's Word and principles and character, the more likely we'll respond correctly in a crisis.

The last time you experienced a crisis, how did you react, more by the flesh or more by the Spirit? If you reacted more by the flesh, why, i.e., in which area do you feel contributed most to your reaction?

In verse 23, Jesus provides an assurance that Lazarus will live again. Martha thinks that Lazarus will live again at the resurrection according to Jewish teaching. But Jesus corrects her and informs her that *He* is the resurrection and the life. The word "life" comes from the Greek word "zoe" which means *the absolute fullness of life*. Jesus is the "absolute fullness of life". Read John 3:16.

Read verses 28 – 32. Notice in verse 32, Mary responds in almost the same way as Martha, with the exception that Mary did not make a declaration of hope in who Jesus is, as Martha did in verse 22.

Jesus Cares About Us

Read verse 33 – 37. The key verse in this passage is verse 33. The Bible says that Jesus "groaned in the spirit" and was "troubled". The phase "groaned in the spirit" means that His feelings were sincere and genuine. The word "troubled" comes from a Greek word "tarasso" which means:

- To disquiet or make restless, to take away his calmness of mind.

Now Jesus knew exactly what He was going to do in this situation. So how is it that Martha, Mary and those who were mourning "took away His calmness of mind"? The answer is that Jesus feels what we feel. He has empathy towards us. He knows exactly what we are feeling. And if He didn't care, He wouldn't be "troubled". Verse 35 expresses a "quiet" shedding of tears. If He didn't care, He wouldn't "weep" for us. Jesus cares about us.

Read I Peter 5:6 – 7.

Key Point: Jesus cares for you and can feel your pain. You are not forgotten.

Have you ever been in the midst of a crisis or a very sad situation, but felt the presence of God with you? Have you ever looked back and realized that you responded to a crisis in a way that even surprised you, i.e., with more peace than you would have had years earlier?

Read verses 37 – 45. An important verse in this passage is verse 39. Lazarus' body had begun to decay. He could not be any more "dead" than he was. Some Jews believed that the soul remained near the body for three days after death with a possibility of reentering the body. But after four days, the body was "dead".

There are times when our situations seem lifeless. Like there is no hope. But we must remember that Jesus *is* the resurrection. If He tells us through His Word or Spirit not to give up hope, then we are not to give up hope.

A word of caution: We may run the danger of "hoping" when there is no "real" hope, because of our strong feelings or desire to have a situation turn out the way we want. We will be driven more by our emotions than direct instructions from God. Jesus told Martha and Mary explicitly that Lazarus would rise again. Their hope wasn't founded on their emotionally driven desire to have their brother back, but by the direct word from Jesus, with whom they had a close relationship. We must be careful that our "extended hope" is directed from the Lord. Sometimes there are thin lines between faith, foolishness and presumption. The key to hearing clearly from the Lord is to have a current, close, intimate relationship with Him.

In verse 43, Jesus spoke and Lazarus came alive. Re-read verse 4. Jesus gave us the key to this entire passage in verse 4. The purpose of His delay and Lazarus' death was for His glory and the Father's. The sickness did not end in death like He said. The result of Lazarus' resurrection is found in verse 45...*many believed in Him*.

Summary

Nothing is beyond our Lord - nothing. In this lesson we have seen several aspects of God's character revealed through Christ:

- He cares for us
- He works on His own time
- He feels what we feel. Our hurts "trouble" Him.
- He is a God of compassion
- He sees and works off of the "big picture", not the scene of the moment.

Read Isaiah 55:8 – 11. God's ways are beyond us. So we can't base our relationship on our circumstances. It is God's character in which we put our faith. The result of Jesus doing things the way He did was that many, many people came to believe in Him. The result of God working in our lives should have the same result – many, by observing us, should come to believe in Him, in addition to the growth of our own faith.

The word "believe" used in John 11:45 comes from a Greek word whose root means:

- to trust and to have confidence in, "to tranquillize"

Our goal as Christians is to daily build up our relationship with God so that we remain "tranquil" in the midst of every storm, and for us to say, "Lord, no matter what, I'll always love You and trust You."

Notes:

_____

_____

_____

_____

_____

_____

_____

_____

_____

_____

_____

_____

_____

_____

_____

_____

_____

_____

_____

_____

_____

_____

_____

_____

_____

_____

_____

Lord I've Blown It – What Now? : Restoration

Introduction

Every person has "blown it" at least once in their life. We can all think of decisions we've made, we later regretted, which had an adverse effect on us and others around us. Perhaps we lied about something, became a parent before we were married, stole something, cheated on our spouses, mistreated our kids, disrespected our parents, ignored sound advice, took the wrong job, or were just lazy. Whatever the action, the results were the same – regrets, pain, discomfort, sadness, hardship.

These types of setbacks can make us feel like we can't be helped by the Lord; we are beyond hope. We may feel like our "mistakes" had consequences so bad, that we have totally destroyed any good plan for our lives. Fortunately, there is something called the Grace of God which is based upon the Love of God which surpasses all understanding. There is hope.

This lesson is a study in the life of a murderer whom God used ultimately to glorify His name. This man committed an act of premeditated murder before the watchful eye of a righteous God. He repented, and through obedience and trust, God glorified His name through this man. If God can forgive murderers and use them for His glory, He can use us too. There is hope of restoration.

Scriptures Used In This Lesson

Exodus 2:11 – 15
Romans 8:1 – 2
Romans 8:1
Philippians 4:7 – 9
Romans 8:15 – 17
2 Corinthians 5:17 – 19
Romans 8:38 – 39

Nobody Was Looking

The life of the "murderer" we'll study is in the book of Exodus. We are all familiar with the latter part of his life, with God performing miracle after miracle. But he made a big "mistake" in the early part of his life. His name is Moses.

In Exodus 1, the king of Egypt had given an order to the Hebrew midwives to kill all male children after they were born. In Exodus 2, we discover that Moses' parents hid him from the Egyptians to protect him. Eventually he was found by Pharaoh's daughter and raised in Pharaoh's house as a prince of Egypt.

When Moses was about 40 years old, he saw an Egyptian beating a Hebrew slave. Read Exodus 2:11 – 15. Notice in verse 12, the Bible says:

> "And he looked this way and that, and when he saw that there was no man, he slew the Egyptian and hid him in the sand." (KJV)

The fact that Moses "looked this way and that", indicates that he gave forethought to the killing of the Egyptian. He wanted to be sure that no one saw what he was about to do. Giving "forethought" to an action with the intent to carry out that action is by definition "premeditation". Moses even hid the body in the sand in an effort to cover up his crime.

One of the sayings I used to hear from my mother is:

> "What's done in the dark will come to the light."

Meaning, if you're doing something you should not be doing, it will be revealed eventually. This was certainly true in Moses' case. In spite of his careful efforts to conceal his crime, someone saw him. When word of his crime eventually got back to Pharaoh, he tried to have Moses killed. So Moses ran for his life into the desert, where he eventually settled in Midian for 40 years.

The consequences of his crime were many. They are not explicitly detailed in the Bible, but we can imagine that they may have included:

- The grieving family and friends of the murder victim
- The guilt associated with committing a murder
- Moses running for his life as a criminal
- Pharaoh's anger and feeling of betrayal by Moses, who was raised in his household
- The shock, sadness, and despair of Moses' biological and adoptive family members
- Having to live in the desert alone
- Living with the fear of being discovered by the Egyptians
- Living with the fear of being confronted by bandits in the desert
- Being faced with trying to stay alive while traveling to Midian
- Feelings of regret and despair of losing all the "good things" he had in life

In one day Moses went from having all the riches of the royal family to the poverty of a homeless criminal. One decision changed his life forever.

Can you think of a decision you or someone else made that was a life changing event, in an unpleasant way? Did you or they think about the possible consequences before the decision was made? How did you/they respond when met with the unpleasant consequences? How did others respond around you/them? What drove you/them to make that decision?

Can you relate to any of these? Is there uncertainty about your future because of one of your actions? Is it difficult to face your parents, friends, and family because of your "mistake"?

Key Point: Rarely do we think about the consequences of our actions before and while we are engaged in "the act".

Key Point: You can't control the severity of the consequences of our actions.

Key Point: The consequences of our actions are usually more severe and far reaching than we anticipate. Many times the consequences will affect not only us, but our family and friends.

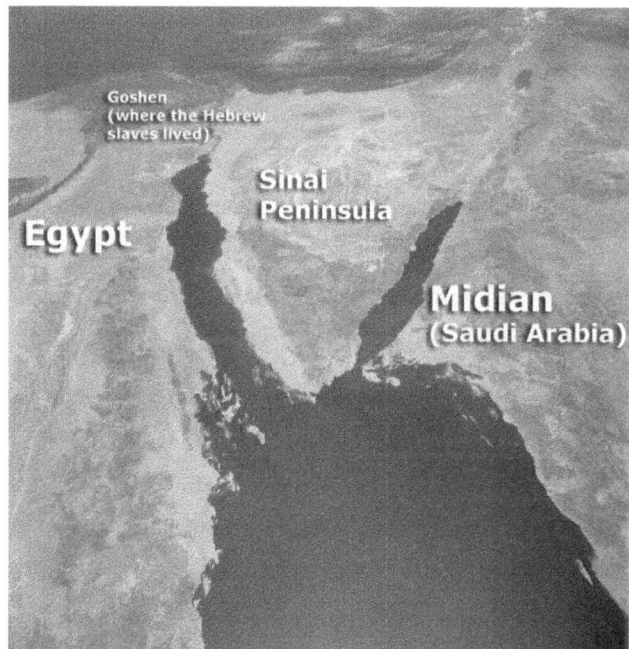

The Desert

The Bible says that Moses ran from Egypt and settled in Midian. Now Midian was approximately 300 miles from Egypt, "as the crow flies". Traveling around the Sinai Peninsula close to water meant walking a distance close to 400 miles. Several deserts exist between Egypt and Midian (which is in current day Saudi Arabia) - the Desert of Shur, the Desert of Paran, The Desert of Sin, and the Desert of Sinai. To say the least, Moses' journey to Midian was not easy.

For us, the desert represents the "post-sin" period. It is the time where we come face to face with the reality of our sin. We experience the consequences of our sins (sin being those things which tend to separate us from God). In our minds we often view it as a time of punishment, a time of regret, a time of sadness, a time of embarrassment. We suffer greatly in the desert, sometimes physically, emotionally, and financially. Most often our suffering is not confined to ourselves; it even touches the ones we love the most.

But for the Christian, *the desert should be a place of transition from despair to restoration.* It is a time where we can get back in right relationship with God; a time of humility and repentance; a turning around. How is it that we can "turn around" and get back right with God when we feel so bad and the consequences of our actions are upon us? Our response to the situation is the key.

Key Point: Many times our feelings about a situation can distort our perspective.

> *Have you ever had an experience where you realized that your emotions did not reflect the reality of a situation?*

We must be aware of certain facts about our relationship with God that have nothing to do with our feelings. Read Romans 8:1 – 2. As a Christian, you are not condemned to eternal death and separation by God because of your actions. There are consequences, for sure, but God doesn't want to push you away and separate you from Himself.

In Roman society when a man was "condemned", he was put to death and separated from everything that was living because of his crime. In God's kingdom, we have been set free from "death" (eternal separation from God) by the Holy Spirit through the death, burial, and resurrection of Christ. We are forgiven and accepted by God. The purpose of Christ coming into the world was to restore the relationship between God and man. Read 2 Corinthians 5:17 – 21.

Read Romans 8:11. For the Christian, we must remember that the Holy Spirit dwells in our hearts. He is the inmost life of God. He is the very power of God. And if He can raise Christ from the grave, He can certainly revitalize our minds, bodies, and emotions. The word "quicken" in the KJV comes from the Greek word "zoopoieo" which means to revitalize, to make alive. So when you feel that your life and future are "dead", remember the fact that the Spirit of God can "quicken" you.

Stay Out of the Moat

During the Middle Ages in Europe, moats were built around castles and other structures as a means of protection. Moats were usually large deep water-filled ditches that prevented people from crossing over into the castle.

When we make "big mistakes", it is easy to fall into the "moat of despair" and never cross over to into restoration. Feelings of depression, regret, guilt, and anger are common. If we let our minds continually dwell on our "mistakes" and their consequences, and let these feelings persist, we can easily become consumed by them. In addition, stress will begin to adversely affect our health.

In order to "stay out of the moat", we have to make a decision; a decision to act upon the facts of our relationship with God. As stated earlier, feelings may be real, but may not reflect reality.

The reality of being a Christian is that the blood of Jesus covers our sins. His blood covers every sin we have committed and will ever commit. God's forgiveness is available to cover all who confess and accept the work of Christ. God doesn't continually "beat us over the head" with reminders of our sins. His goal is to conform or shape us into the likeness of Christ in our character and actions. This can't be done if we continually "waddle in the moat of despair".

So how do we stay out of the moat? Part of the answer comes from Philippians 4:7 – 9. Instead of thinking about the bad, we need to think about good or positive things. Whatever becomes the focus of our minds, becomes the dominate force in our daily lives. If we think on things that are good (like the grace of God), then His grace will influence our daily lives.

Key Point: Whatever becomes the focus of our minds, becomes the dominate force in our daily lives. The more we think about a thing, the bigger it becomes in our minds.

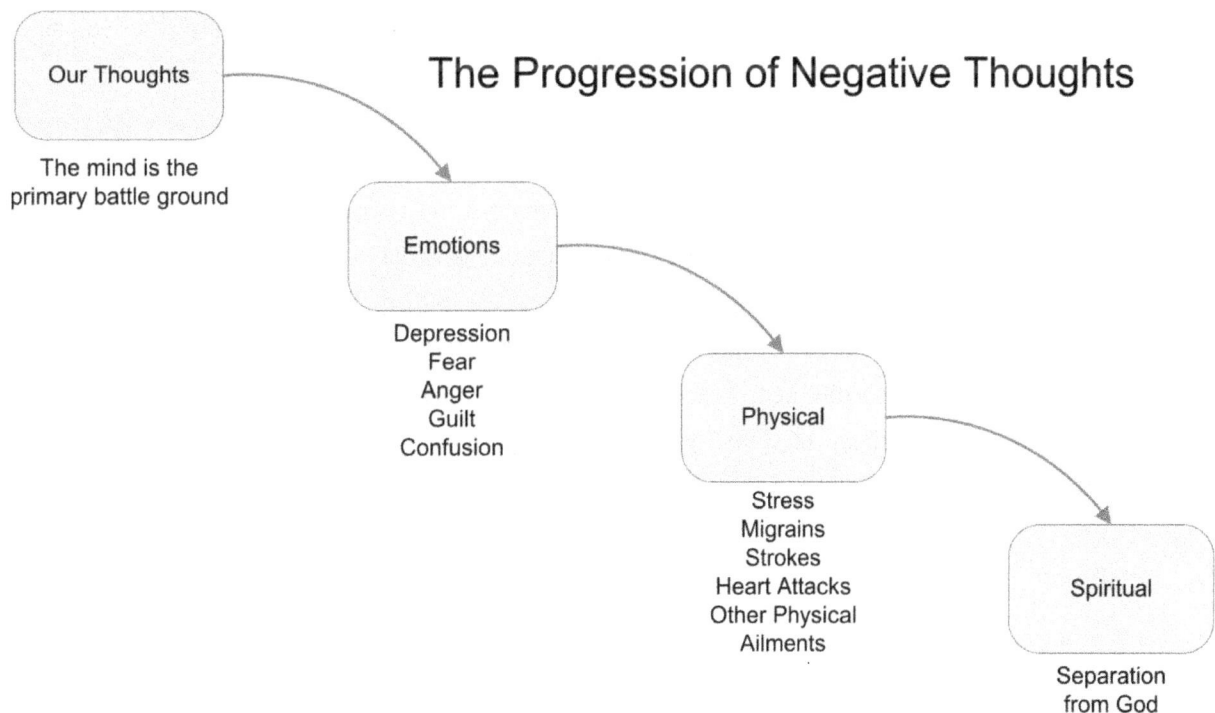

The Progression of Negative Thoughts

Our Thoughts

The mind is the
primary battle ground

Emotions

Depression
Fear
Anger
Guilt
Confusion

Physical

Stress
Migrains
Strokes
Heart Attacks
Other Physical
Ailments

Spiritual

Separation
from God

Staying out of the moat is more than just positive thinking. It is focusing and meditating on the truths of God's promises and character. It involves reading about Joseph in the book of Genesis and seeing how God restored him after a decade of trials and tribulation. It's thinking about how God will work in your life like He did in Joseph's. It's reading Psalms 27 imagining how David felt when he wrote it. It's picturing how he looked up at the sky to "see" the Lord and making a decision to wait upon Him. It's making a similar decision in your life to wait upon the Lord. It's filling your mind on God's faithfulness and love for you. It's realizing that His love for you is not based on your performance; it's based on His unchanging character. These are the facts that keep us out of the moat of despair.

Key Point: God's love for you is not based on your performance; it is based on His unchanging character.

Restoration

Read Romans 8:15 – 17. When you accepted Christ as your Savior, you became a child of God. God meant for this relationship to be intimate. Verse 15 says that by the Holy Spirit we cry out, "Abba, Father". "Abba" was used in Middle Eastern languages as we use "Daddy" in English. "Daddy" denotes closeness, intimacy, and a personal relationship.

By the Holy Spirit (Whom you received when you accepted Christ), you can call God - "Daddy", *even after you sin*. This is important. He was "Daddy" before you sinned and He is "Daddy" after you sin.

Key Point: God is "Daddy" all the time.

The great thing about "Daddy" is that He wants to restore the relationship between you and He. That's been His desire since Adam and Eve. Read 2 Corinthians 5:17 – 21.

Through Christ, we have been "reconciled" to God. By definition, we have been "returned to favor" with God. Our sinfulness has been "exchanged" for the righteousness of Christ. *Understand and accept the fact that because of Christ, you are in right standing with God.* Daddy still loves you; nothing can separate you from His love – nothing. Read Romans 8:38 – 39.

Key Point: "Daddy" loves you all the time.

So the facts of the matter are: 1) God desires to restore the relationship between you and He, even after your sin, 2) Christ died to make that possible, and 3) the Holy Spirit, Who dwells in you, is the power that seals that restoration.

So whether you "feel" restored or not, by the shed blood of Christ, you are restored.

What are some ways you can help others who are so focused on their current circumstances that they don't see the facts?

What are some ways you can help others who are so caught up with the regrets of the past? What helped you the most? Based on the "facts", what is the best way to deal with the past?

Key Point: Focus on the facts, not your feelings.

So What's The Next Step?

God took the first step in your restoration by establishing the plan. Christ took the second step by dying on the cross. The Holy Spirit took the third step by bringing your restoration to pass when you accepted Christ in your heart. These are the facts that you accept and live by. The next steps for you are:

- Make daily efforts to "know" God on a personal level. Seek Him with your whole heart - not blessing, needs, desires, or what He can do for you, but Him *first*.

- Confess any known sin to Him and ask Him to forgive you and deliver you from any strongholds, like bitterness, bad habits, etc. You may need to forgive yourself.

- Ask Him to glorify His name in your life – from wherever you are, with whatever you have at that moment, ask Him to use you for His glory.

- Be obedient to His leading and trust Him to take care of the details.

Our personal relationship with God, through Christ, by the Holy Spirit is the key to our turnaround.

Summary

In Exodus 3, we read about Moses' burning bush experience that changed his life forever. God glorified His name through Moses so that people 40 years later were still fearful of Him and His power (Joshua 2:8 – 13). God can do the same for you. God is waiting to restore a right relationship with you and the opportunity to glorify His name. He just needs you to say, "Yes, Lord, here am I".

Notes:

_____

_____

_____

_____

_____

_____

_____

_____

_____

_____

_____

_____

_____

_____

_____

_____

_____

_____

_____

_____

_____

_____

_____

_____

_____

_____

_____

_____

God's Faithfulness: What Does It Mean?

Introduction

The book of Joshua is really the culmination of God's promise to Abraham, as depicted in Genesis 12, 13, 15 and 17. As I read the book recently, one aspect of God's character kept speaking to me: "God is faithful". As I thought about it, I had some questions: Didn't Abraham, to whom God made the Promised Land covenant, die hundreds of years before Joshua and the Israelites entered the Promised Land? Didn't Israel's sin cause them to wander in the desert for 40 years and delay the fulfillment of the promise? Didn't Joshua and the Israelites have to fight for their land once they got there? Why didn't God allow Abraham to enjoy the "milk and the honey"?

I realized that my expectation of how God would keep the promise to Abraham was different than the reality of what happened. In fact, my expectation of how God will answer my prayers is usually different than what He does. And I think this is what causes many Christians to give up their faith in God and doubt Him during troublesome times.

This lesson is a study in God's faithfulness and our expectations. The goal is to better understand the character of God so that our faith does not waver during difficult times.

Scriptures Used in This Lesson

Psalm 36:5

Psalm 100:5

Psalm 143:1

Genesis 12:2 – 3, 6 – 7

Genesis 15:1 – 21

Genesis 17:1 – 8, 15 – 22

Romans 8:29

Joshua 24:1 – 4, 11 – 13

Faithfulness – What Does It Mean?

One of the key attributes of God's character that every Christian must understand is His faithfulness. The Bible clearly and repeatedly declares God's faithfulness. Here are just a few passages:

Psalm 36:5

Thy mercy, O LORD, is in the heavens; and thy faithfulness reacheth unto the clouds.

(this verse expresses that the extent of God's faithfulness is great)

Psalm 100:5

For the LORD is good; his mercy is everlasting; and his truth endureth to all generations.

(the word *truth* is the same Hebrew word translated *faithfulness* in Psalm 36:5, *'emuwnah*)

Psalm 143:1

Hear my prayer, O LORD, give ear to my supplications: in thy faithfulness answer me, and in thy righteousness.

But what exactly does it mean that God is faithful, especially as it pertains to our daily lives? The Hebrew word used in these passages and others in the Old Testament is 'emuwnah. The word means:

Firmness, fidelity, steadfastness, steadiness

Today, when we use the word "fidelity", we usually think of "quality", as in *high fidelity stereo*. But fidelity actually means:

- The quality or state of being faithful
- Accuracy in details: exactness

Fidelity:

"implies strict and continuing faithfulness to an obligation, trust, or duty"

These definitions are important for us as we enter each new day. God is strict and continually faithful to his Word. By reading how God's faithfulness was revealed in Abraham's life, we can better understand how His faithfulness can be revealed in our lives. Let's read God's promise to Abraham. Read Genesis 12:2 – 3, 6 – 7, 15:1 – 21.

The covenant between God and Abraham (and his descendants) is presented in detail in these passages. God spoke to Abram(ham) on several occasions around 2100 BC. In Genesis 15, Abraham's expectation was that Eliezer, his servant, would be his heir, since he and his wife were childless. But God told him "a son coming from your own body will be your heir" (Gen. 15:4). Then God did something interesting to give Abram an idea of the magnitude of the promise. Read verse 15:5.

Have you ever been out camping or out in a rural area on a clear night? The sky is full of stars. Some parts of the sky have so many stars that it looks "cloudy". As a child, I used to wonder, "Man...where did all these stars come from?" I was overwhelmed by the magnitude of what I saw.

While viewing the sky from inside a city, your vision is obscured by the city lights which surround you. At best, you can see just a handful of only the brightest stars. But out in the country, without the city lights to interfere with your vision, you see that the sky is full of stars.

Just as the city lights interfere with our vision of the stars in the sky, the daily trails of life can obscure our "vision" of God's faithfulness. The city lights are analogous to the concerns and activities of daily life. We get so focused on work, school, family, friends, bills, relationships, and life's daily issues that we lose sight of God's big picture in our lives, as well as His daily, continual blessings. In a sense, we can't see God's "bigness"; many times, we can't see God at all.

Key Point: We are prevented from seeing God and His faithfulness many times because we are consumed with life's daily issues.

There are several reason why we get "blinded by the city lights", i.e., consumed by life's daily issues. A few of these are listed below:

Emotions: The more emotional we are about a situation or person, the harder it is see God. Worry, anger, and fear are common. Uncertainty, which is really a lack of confidence in God, can open the door to a number of other emotions, the most powerful of which is fear.

Pride: Many times we think, "I can handle this on my own.", and bypass God. We ignore the fact that we may not know all the facts or that God may want us to handle the situation in a manner different than which we are inclined. Pride, based on our perceived intellectual abilities, can also "blind us".

Lack of Relationship: If we have been lax in our personal relationship with the Lord, we will have a tendency to respond more "out of the flesh" as opposed to "out of the Spirit". (You can't trust whom you don't know).

Lack of Knowledge: If we don't know biblical principles, then we don't know His ways. If we don't understand His ways, then we will "miss Him" as He works in our lives. (Lack of knowledge is really related to our relationship with Him).

<u>Disbelief</u>: Belief in God is critical in seeing His hand in your life. If you don't believe that God will work on your behalf or He is in control, you will miss Him all together.

<u>Disobedience</u>: If you are willfully acting in disobedience to God, His Word, or His Ways, it's like putting on sunglasses at night...there is no way you will see the "stars of His faithfulness".

> *Which one of the above has recently "obscured your vision of God"? Why? What did it take for you to finally see God? Can you think of other things which can "obscure your vision" of God working in your daily issues?*

When Abraham looked up at the sky as God commanded, he saw millions upon millions of stars, and understood that what God had promised him was "big"...very big. And then Abraham did something remarkable that changed his entire life. Read Genesis 15:6.

Abraham believed God...he took God at His Word.

> *Do you think Abraham understood how God was going to keep His promise? Approximately how old were Abraham and Sarah at the time? Is it common for people that old to have children? <u>What do you think Abraham's belief in God was based upon, i.e., why do you think he believed God?</u>*

The last question is an important question for all of us...why did Abraham believe God? And more importantly, what keeps us from believing God? Think about it...God shows us His glory (things which only He can receive credit) everyday. We experience it in the form of comfort, food, shelter, clothing, family, the air we breathe, the fact that we are still alive today, past miracles, as well as many others – these are the "stars" in our lives, and we don't believe He can handle our present situation.

Abraham had less than we have, as a "believer". He had the presence of God and the stars in the sky. We have past blessings, His Indwelling Spirit, His Word (the Bible), preachers, and teachers...and we still don't see the stars sometimes.

> *What keeps us from believing God like Abraham did in Genesis 15:6?*

Expectations
Many times we lose faith in a faithful God because He doesn't meet our expectations. During times of trials, we want to get out of our "mess" as quickly as possible. We don't want to feel any pain or

discomfort; we want immediate gratification. *So we expect God to move on our behalf quickly.* And herein lays the problem.

Our anticipation of God's movement is, "Now." We don't want to wait. The longer we wait, the longer we suffer. We ignore the fact that God, Who is sovereign, may have a bigger purpose in mind. We ignore the fact the He knows the future and we don't. We ignore the fact that He helped us in the past and is more than capable of helping us now. We want deliverance *now.*

Read Romans 8:29. The Bible says that we are being conformed to the image of Christ. The word "conformed" comes from the Greek word "summorphos" which means "having the same form as another". This "transformation" from "us" to "Christ-likeness" takes time. Some aspects of our nature transform quickly; other aspects take longer. But the key is to know God is faithful, i.e., He has a *strict and continuing faithfulness to an obligation, trust, or duty* to us as His children.

Just as our children sometimes have to wait for what is best for them, we sometimes have to wait for God's best for us.

Key Point: Sometimes we have to wait for God's best and/or for Him to fulfill His purpose in our lives.

> *Why don't children like to wait? Why don't we (adults) like to wait? What can help us be more patient?*

Another area where our expectations are not met involves the "object of our faith". We become disappointed with God and miss His faithfulness because the object of our faith is "God acting quickly" as opposed to "God having a *strict and continuing faithfulness to an obligation, trust, or duty* to us as His children, i.e., "time" verses God's character. And this leads to disappointment.

Key Point: Having faith in anything other than God's character or Word, will lead to disappointment.

Key Point: God moves on our behalf based on His character, purpose, and His love.

I recently came out of a season in my life that consisted of a series of serious trials and tribulations that lasted over 10 years. I couldn't not see "the end of the tunnel". I did not know when God would deliver me. I finally came to a point where I had to decide to trust in God's character (and Word) as opposed to my desired timing for deliverance. Everyday turned into a decision to trust God - not a feeling, but a *decision.*

Now I am in a season of blessings and God showed Himself to be faithful…again.

Abraham's descendents finally conquered and settled in the Promised Land under Joshua's leadership (Joshua 24:1 – 4, 11 – 13). Joshua lived around 1400 BC. God, made His promise to Abraham around 2100 BC. So God remained faithful to a promise He made 700 years earlier.

Think about it – Abraham, Isaac, and Jacob had all died long before the Israelites settled in the Promised Land. There was no one alive who directly heard the Promise. But God's nature involves a _strict and continuing faithfulness to an obligation, trust, or duty_ to His children. He remained faithful and kept His promise.

Summary

God loves you. Don't give up on Him during times of trials. Have faith in His character and Word, which never change. Trust in Him, not your timeframe, and one day you will see the goodness of your Heavenly Father revealed in your life.

Notes:

_____

_____

_____

_____

_____

_____

_____

_____

_____

_____

_____

_____

_____

_____

_____

_____

_____

_____

_____

_____

_____

_____

_____

_____

_____

_____

_____

_____

Sweet and Sour: A "Verse 18" Attitude

Introduction

Have you ever been through a difficult period in your life, but have seen the hand of God working on your behalf in the midst of it? Did you feel like you were being blessed and punished at the same time? Well, I've just gone through a situation like this and I wondered, "What is going on? I can see God blessing me in some areas of my life, but my circumstances haven't changed yet. Things are still kind of 'sour'." My expectation was, "God was going to get me out of my circumstance *immediately* since He was blessing me. Then things would be 'sweet'."

This lesson will help us to better understand how God operates during these "sweet and sour" situations, i.e., where we see the hand of God working on our behalf, but have not received a *quick* deliverance from our circumstances. Also it will instruct us on how to respond during these times, i.e., to offer praise in the midst of the fire.

Scriptures Used in This Lesson

Genesis 39

Romans 8:28

Genesis 41:16, 25, 28

Genesis 45:1 – 11

Genesis 41:50 – 52

Daniel 3

Background

There are two stories that are relevant to our "sweet and sour" situation. They are the story of Joseph and the story of Shadrach, Meshach and Abednego. The first story is a familiar one and takes place primarily in Egypt. Joseph was born approximately 1900 years before Christ. He was the eleventh of twelve sons born to Jacob, and was his father's favorite. Due to their jealousy, Joseph was sold as a slave by his brothers and ended up as a servant in the house of Potiphar, an official of Pharaoh, the king of Egypt. Most of the background is found in Genesis 37. For our purposes, the story begins in Genesis 39.

Sour...and then Sweet

Read Genesis 39:1 – 6. If you're not careful, you can miss some rather important points in this passage because they are presented in just a few short verses. Joseph, at 17 years old, had suffered greatly. He was stripped of a prized gift his father had given him, the coat of many colors. He suffered the physical pain of being thrown down a dry well (Genesis 37:23 – 24). He experienced the shock and fear knowing that his brothers wanted to kill him. He was stripped of his dignity by being sold as a slave, suffered betrayal, and was forcibly taken over three hundred miles from his home to Egypt.

In Egypt, Potiphar was not only an official of Pharaoh, he was captain of Pharaoh's guard. Escape from slavery was unlikely for Joseph. Was God in control of his life? Yes. Did God allow all this to happen to him? Yes. Did God turn His back on Joseph? No. Joseph's situation was very "sour". But in the midst these hard times, God made Joseph's situation "sweet", i.e., He blessed Joseph by showing him favor.

Verse 29:2 says three things: 1) the Lord was with Joseph, 2) Joseph prospered, and 3) Joseph was a slave in the house of Potiphar. Now, I thought about this and wondered, "How in the world can you be a slave and prosper? How can you say, 'God is with you', when you're suffering? How can this situation be 'sweet' and 'sour' at the same time?" We'll address these questions in a minute.

Have you ever been in a "sour" situation but saw the hand of God blessing you? How did you feel about God? Did the blessings encourage you, confuse you, or did it take some time before you noticed them?

Key Point: When we are in the midst of a "sour" situation, the blessing we're looking for (complete, quick deliverance) may not be the blessing that God immediately provides.

Why do you think the Key Point above is true? What does it say about God? What does it say about us? Read Romans 8:28.

Read Genesis 39:7 – 23. Here we have Joseph suffering at the hand of Potiphar's wife. He ignored her advances, she lied about him, and he ended up in prison. But verse 9 is a key verse. Who did Joseph acknowledge as the one whom he couldn't sin against, Potiphar or God? It was God. This is revealing. This indicates that Joseph, in spite of all that he had endured, in spite of what God had allowed to happen, had a desire in his heart not to sin against God. It was Potiphar's wife around whom the controversy revolved, but Joseph acknowledged that the sin would have been against God first. This is indicative of the God-Joseph relationship still being intact, in spite of the circumstances.

In your "sour" situation, did your relationship with God change? If so, how? Why did it change?

Verse 21 is another key verse. It says: 1) the Lord was with Joseph, 2) the Lord showed him kindness, and 3) the Lord granted him favor with the warden. God was adding "sweetness" to a "sour" situation.

Forgotten, But Not Forgotten

Genesis 40 tells us how Joseph interpreted the dreams of two of Pharaoh's servants. One of the servants was going to die and the other would be freed from prison and return to Pharaoh's service. Joseph appealed to the servant who would live to remember him and ask Pharaoh to get him out of prison. But the chapter ended with Joseph being forgotten for two years.

A key verse in Genesis 40 is verse 8. Joseph acknowledges that interpretations to dreams belong to God. This indicates that his relationship with God was still intact, even after he had been in prison for some time. The same indication is given in Chapter 41:16, 25, 28.

After the two year period, Pharaoh had a dream and Joseph was called upon to interpret the dream. Joseph acknowledged God in his responses to the king. This is especially significant given the fact that Joseph had been captive for 13 years up to this time.

God allowed Joseph to be held captive for 13 years, due to no fault of his own. *But God had a purpose.* Remember Romans 8:28. The last part of the verse indicates that God has a purpose for us who are called. And Joseph was one who was called by God.

Genesis 41 tells us that Joseph was freed from prison after interpreting Pharaoh's dream. Pharaoh was so impressed with Joseph's "wisdom" that he put Joseph in charge of running the affairs of all of Egypt. Not only was he free, but Joseph was second only to Pharaoh in Egypt, the land of his captivity. God made his life "sweet".

Looking back we can see how God prepared Joseph for this position. As a slave in Potiphar's house, Joseph learned to run a small household. As a prisoner, Joseph increased his skills and learned to run the affairs of a larger organization, a prison. The prison experience prepared Joseph for the ultimate duty of running Egypt. The 13 years of imprisonment may have seemed like God had forgotten Joseph, but He hadn't; *God was preparing Joseph for His purpose.*

The Ultimate Purpose Revealed

Joseph's ultimate purpose was not revealed until 9 years later, when Joseph made himself known to his brothers. Read Genesis 45:1 – 11. Joseph realized and revealed to his brothers the hand of God in all that had happened. God fulfilled Romans 8:28 nineteen hundred years before it was written by

Paul; God had a plan for Joseph that involved 13 years of "sour" living. But God made it "sweet"; He made is so "sweet" that Joseph forgot all his troubles in Egypt. Read Genesis 41:50 – 52.

Key Point: God's purpose for our lives can take years to develop, but His loving hand is never far away.

Have you been in a "sour" situation that you later realized that God was fulfilling His purpose for your life? Knowing what you know now, what would you do differently if you were in that same situation again?

God in His goodness provides us with "sweets" throughout our "sour" situation until His purpose in our lives is fulfilled. The "sweets" are signs of encouragement to let us know that He is with us, He is in control, and for us not to faint. They are also signs of His power and influence. If we continually focus on the "sweets" and what they represent, we will be triumphant during the "sour" times.

How Should We Respond When Life is "Sour"?
We Need A "Verse 18" Attitude!
It is evident in the life of Joseph that he kept his relationship with the Lord intact during the 13 "sour" years. We should do the same during the "sour" times of our lives. A very clear illustration of this is found in Daniel 3, the story of Shadrach, Meshach and Abednego. Read Daniel 3.

The three had already been given high positions in the Babylonian government (Daniel 2:48 – 49). Nebuchadnezzar demanded that people worship the idol he had made of himself. The three "Hebrew boys" would not. Re-read Daniel 3:13 – 18; these verses illustrate a critical point, especially verse 18. They did not know for sure if God would deliver them. They knew He was able, but did not know their ultimate fate. The fire was real; Nebuchadnezzar's anger was real; the death of soldiers holding them was real. They were in a very "sour" situation. They were actually thrown in the fire. *But their faithfulness to God was the key to their victory*, as verse 18 testifies.

The three "Hebrew boys" were not delivered from the fire, but in the *midst* of the fire.

Key Point: God's deliverance may come *after* you've been thrown in the fire, not before. But this serves to demonstrate His power all the more.

We look for deliverance from hard times, but sometimes God receives more glory after we're in the fire. To survive our trials and to give Him glory, we need a "verse 18" attitude; no matter how things turn out, we will serve the Lord. This is how we should respond to the "sour" situations in our lives.

So if you get the call that your son was arrested, you need a "verse 18" attitude; only God can turn that situation around. If you get a call from the doctor and you've have to have surgery performed, you need a "verse 18" attitude; only God can turn that situation around. If your bills are more than your income, you need a "verse 18"; only God can turn that situation around.

A "verse 18" attitude is for life, not for the moment. Remember God's purpose may take years to fulfill. But He will provide you with encouragement ("sweets") to help keep your faith strong.

Summary – Making It Real

It's good to have an understanding of what God is doing in your life. It helps provide a level of peace inside. It's nice to have some scriptures to read to help keep yourself in a positive frame of mind. But there are times when you'll be in the fire and you'll see flames all around you. It will be easy to become fearful thinking about all the what-if's of your situation. You can become discouraged with the receipt of another bill you can't pay. You can become sadden with another phone call. How can you hold on and live with a "verse 18" attitude?

1. Make a choice – a choice to trust God no matter what happens. There is no other place to go. He may work through other people, but God is your ultimate source.

2. Prayer. Right after you get that letter or phone call, pray. First acknowledge God for who He is and remind yourself of what He has done for you. Thank Him for the blessings you've received in the past (name them, at least five). Then tell Him of the situation or need. After that, thank Him for His faithfulness and that He will work in your behalf.

3. Pray Some More. Prayer keeps the communication line opened between you and God. It helps keep you in a "God-frame-of-mind". Talk to Him throughout the day. Thank Him. Praise Him. Ask Him for guidance. Tell Him how you feel. Ask for wisdom.

4. Read His Word. Reading the Word keeps your mind on Him and not on the what-if's of your situation. It also gives the Holy Spirit an opportunity to talk to you or more correctly, it puts you in a state where you can hear what He's saying.

5. Act As He Directs – Sometimes the Lord may put someone in your path who may encourage you, provide temporary relief, or will help you in the final deliverance/solution. The Lord may want you to act, or He may want you to wait. But remember that He will never leave you nor forsake you.

Notes:

_____

_____

_____

_____

_____

_____

_____

_____

_____

_____

_____

_____

_____

_____

_____

_____

_____

_____

_____

_____

_____

_____

_____

_____

_____

Can You Be Sure?

Introduction

"Can you be sure that you're going to Heaven after you die? Can you be sure that you're saved? How do you know that you believe in Jesus enough to be saved?" These questions are at the very heart of Christianity, and unfortunately many Christians struggle with the answers. God sacrificed His Only Son so that our relationship with Him could be restored. The last thing He would want would be for us to be uncertain or confused about that relationship, especially after making such a great sacrifice. Fortunately, we can be sure.

This lesson is designed to answer these questions and provide you with a foundation for you to be sure about "what you know" based on the scriptures.

Scriptures Used In This Lesson

Mark 16:15 – 16

Luke 8:11 – 15

Acts 16:25 – 34

Romans 10:8 – 10

Ephesians 1:13

I John 4:13 -15

I John 3:24

John 14:17

Galatians 4:6

I John 2:23

To Believe

Believing in Jesus Christ is at the core of salvation. Read the following scriptures:

Mark 16:15 – 16

Luke 8:1 – 15

Acts 16:25 – 34 (in particular verses 30 – 31)

Romans 10:8 – 10

But, what does it mean to believe? Does simply voicing the words mean that you believe something or is there more? In the New Testament the Greek word most commonly used in association with salvation, that is translated "believe" is "pisteuo". The word means:

- to think to be true, to be persuaded of, to credit, place confidence in

- to trust in Jesus or God as able to aid either in obtaining or in doing something: saving faith

When we truly "believe" something to be true, that belief affects our actions. An illustration I commonly use is as follows:

Supposed there is a chair in a room which you believe the front two legs have been sawed to the point where they can't support much weight. Would you go and sit in the chair? Why not? What would your thoughts be about the chair?

You would not sit in the chair because you would not want to fall down and hurt yourself. You would perceive the chair to be dangerous. You may even move the chair to a corner of the room and turn it upside down to keep others from sitting on it and hurting themselves. Why would all this take place? Because of your belief. Your belief in the weakness of the legs influenced your thoughts and actions, and even expressed itself in your concern for other people.

If you "believe" in Christ, and that belief influences your actions and thinking, then you know that your belief is real. So the question to ask of yourself is, "Does my belief in Christ have a genuine, daily influence on my thoughts and behavior?" If your answer is "Yes", then you can be sure.

Key Point: True belief in Christ influences your thoughts and behavior.

Key Point: How often, and the degree to which your thinking and behavior is influenced by your belief in Christ, is an indication of your spiritual maturity.

Let's take another look at Luke 8:4 – 15. In this parable, especially in verses 11 – 15, Jesus provides us some additional insight into the belief that leads to salvation. In verse 12, we see that the devil "takes the word away *from their hearts*, so that they may not believe and be saved" (NIV). Believing takes place in your heart, the inmost part of a person. That is why true belief affects your actions and attitudes.

Key Point: Believing takes place in the heart, the inmost part of a person.

Verse 13 talks of those who receive and believe "for a while", but during a time of testing, they fall away, or become faithless. *Two key points given here are: 1) your belief will be tested, and 2) true belief survives testing.* "Belief" that does not survive testing may be more intellectual or emotional in its foundation; it does not penetrate your innermost being, so it's not "true" belief as described in verses 14 and 15.

Verse 14 talks of true belief, but it is "choked" by the cares of this world. So by the standard set in verse 15, it bears little or no fruit. It's important to note that there are Christians who truly are influenced by their belief in Christ, but are not as fruitful as they should because of worry, fear, discouragement, an unbalanced desire for earthly things, etc.

> *How can we help Christians who are discouraged be more fruitful? How about ones who are fearful? How about ones who are coveting earthly things?*

Another test I use to determine if I truly trust God in an area of my life is by asking the question, "How relaxed am I about this situation confronting me?" If I'm fearful or full of worry, then I'm not as fruitful as I should be and fall under verse 14. My goal is to become more like verse 15.

Those Christians, who "walk" in faith and belief, are fruitful in their lives. The "fruit" that God produces in the life of a believing (pisteuo) Christian varies based on their skills or talents, God's purpose, or stage of life. But the point of verse 15 is that God produces fruit in the life of a believing Christian. So if God is producing fruit in your life by you being a godly influence at home or work, or your interceding in prayer for others, or being active in the ministry of your church, and God receives the glory, then you can be sure of your belief.

Key Point: God produces fruit in the life of a believing Christian.

> *Name some other ways God can produce fruit in the life of a Christian.*

Who's Inside Me?
God, in His Grace, provided another way for us to be sure of our salvation, and that's by the Holy Spirit. Read Ephesians 1:13.

The Amplified Bible reads:

> In Him you also who have heard the Word of Truth, the glad tidings (Gospel) of your salvation, and have believed in and adhered to and relied on Him, were stamped with the seal of the long-promised Holy Spirit.

This passages states that first you heard the gospel of your salvation. Next, when you believed (pisteou) the gospel, you received the Holy Spirit. The Holy Spirit is the "witness" inside us Who confirms that we are His Children, i.e., He lives in us and we live in Him. Read I John 4:13 – 15, I John 3:24.

Key Point: The Holy Spirit lets us know that we are His.

Read John 14:17. Where does the Spirit reside? Inside the believing Christian. Read Galatians 4:6. Again, we see that God's Spirit dwells in us, His children. The Spirit testifies that we are His. Things we hear, see or do that are contrary to Jesus, His will or ways, won't "feel" right. Why? Because they go contrary to the Spirit Who dwells in us. Again, we can be sure.

Acknowledging The Son

The key to salvation is in "acknowledging the Son", i.e., Jesus. Read I John 2:23. The key words in this verse are "deny (or denieth)" and "acknowledge (or acknowledgeth)".

The Greek word used for deny is "arneomai", which means:

- to deny
- to deny, abnegate, abjure
- not to accept, to reject, *to refuse something offered*

(Emphasis mine)

The definition that caught my attention was "to refuse something offered". God offered Christ as a living sacrifice for all our sins. It was an offer for us to be restored to right relationship with the Father. When we "deny" Christ, we refuse the offer from God; we refuse to follow or obey or recognize the "Gift from God". To "abjure" means to reject solemnly. There is a thoughtful and willful rejection of Christ.

Now for the other side. The word "acknowledge" comes from the Greek word "homologeo" which means:

- to say the same thing as another, i.e. to agree with, *assent*
- to concede
- not to refuse, to promise
- not to deny
- to confess

- declare
- to confess, i.e. to admit or declare one's self guilty of what one is accused of
- to profess
- to declare openly, speak out freely
- to profess one's self the worshipper of one
- to praise, celebrate

(Emphasis mine)

The word "assent" means to agree with something especially after *thoughtful consideration*. To acknowledge the Son means to accept and agree with Him, especially after thoughtful consideration. Acceptance precludes purely emotional responses. Our acceptance of Christ may involve an emotional experience, especially one of great joy, but it is not based strictly on emotions.

Acknowledgement of Christ is a decision, not a feeling. It is after *thoughtful consideration* that our "beliefs" enter our hearts and take root.

> *After thoughtful consideration, have you accepted Christ? If you have answered, "Yes", then you can be sure.*

Summary

There are many scriptures that address salvation. There is no need for the Christian to be confused about his/her salvation. If we understand that true belief takes place in our hearts and affects our actions, we can be sure. If we understand that we have the Spirit of God living inside us providing affirmation of our relationship with God, we can be sure. If we have given thoughtful consideration to the Gospel and have accepted Christ, then we can be sure. Now we can "boldly" approach the "throne of grace" for anything at anytime of the day or night, because we can be sure.

Notes:

Fear Not

Introduction

Fear is one of our most debilitating emotions we experience. Fear can cause a soldier to turn away from battle; it can cause an athlete to perform at a level far below his/her abilities; it can cause a little child (and their parents) to endure sleepless nights. For the Christian, fear is the result of weakened faith in God and causes us to miss, not only His blessings, but opportunities to draw closer to Him.

Throughout the Bible, our Father told his children to "fear not", sometimes in the midst of very dire circumstances. When they were obedient, they experienced the "glory of God"; miraculous things happened that showed just how powerful He was and how much He was in control.

The goal of this lesson is to teach us how to be less fearful (and as a result more faithful) in the midst of our trials. As a result, we, just like our spiritual forefathers, will experience the "glory of God" in our lives and deepen our personal relationship with our Heavenly Father.

Scriptures Used in This Lesson

Deuteronomy 31:1 – 8

Psalm 23

2 Corinthians 1:3 – 5

Isaiah 42:16

2 Corinthians 1:8 – 10

Exodus 13:20 – 22

Romans 8:35 – 39

Joshua 1:1 – 9

The "Flavors" of Fear

Fear can take on many "flavors" in our lives, i.e., it can manifest itself in a number of ways. Fear can be in the form of apprehension, nervousness, anger, mood swings, or erratic behavior. Sometimes these "flavors" can influence our behavior in subtle ways, while at other times they can be more pronounced. As a result we can find ourselves telling "white lies" to get out of a situation, disappointing others who are depending on us, missing out on opportunities to help others, or losing opportunities for our own advancement. One direction that fear always pushes us towards is disobedience with respect to God's plan, direction, commands, and fellowship.

Now there is a healthy side to fear. In its "mild" state it can influence our behavior such that we are more cautious and thoughtful in our actions. We may tend to be a little more thorough before making a decision. This is a good thing. But in its more pronounced state, fear gets "ugly". It can have a debilitating effect on us, i.e., it can "weaken" our ability to accomplish even simple tasks. A more severe effect is that it can lead us into disobedience as God attempts to lead and guide us by His Spirit; we won't be able to "hear" Him speak.

The Journey of Fear

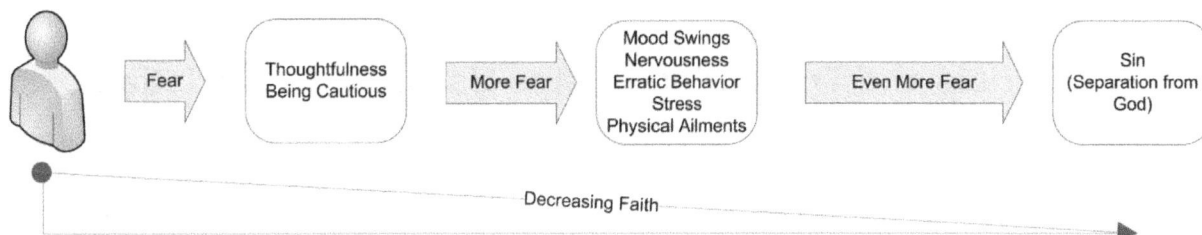

Do you know someone who lives a fearful life? How does living with fear affect them? Worry is a more subtle form of fear. Do you know someone who worries most of the time? How does worry affect them and the ones around them? Would you describe them as a joyful person?

Key Point: Even in its subtle form, fear reduces our faith in God.

Reasons Not To Fear

One of the classic examples of instructions to "fear not", is given in Deuteronomy 31:1 – 8. After 40 years of wandering in the desert, the children of Israel are finally ready to cross over the Jordan River into the Promised Land. Moses, who will not be going with them, passes on leadership to Joshua. The scripture details Moses' instructions to the nation of Israel and Joshua. Verses 6, 7, and 8 provide the basic instructions, "Be strong and courageous", "Do not be afraid", and "do not be discouraged". But what else is given in this passage? *The reasons not to be fearful.*

Read Deuteronomy 31:3. God was going to cross "ahead" of them; they were going to be led by God. This meant that any situation that they encountered was first going to be met by God Himself. How comforting is that?!

As His child, God will go "ahead" of every problem you encounter. If you are in the midst of a trial, He foresaw it and provided a way for you to be victorious *through* it. Usually we want God to deliver us *from* the trial. But sometimes He allows us to go *through* the trial. Read the most famous Psalm - Psalm 23. Where did David walk according to verse 4? *Through* the valley, not around it. But as he walked, was he afraid? No…why? God was with him; David was comforted by the presence of God.

It is *through* the fire that we grow and become more mature as Christians. We develop the skills, wisdom, insight, and strength to help others who may be going through similar types of trials. Read 2 Corinthians 1:3 – 5.

God wants us to be vessels through which He can bless other people. As we trust Him to complete His work through our trials, we become vessels of great blessings for others.

Trials and Tribulations Helps Us Grow As Christians

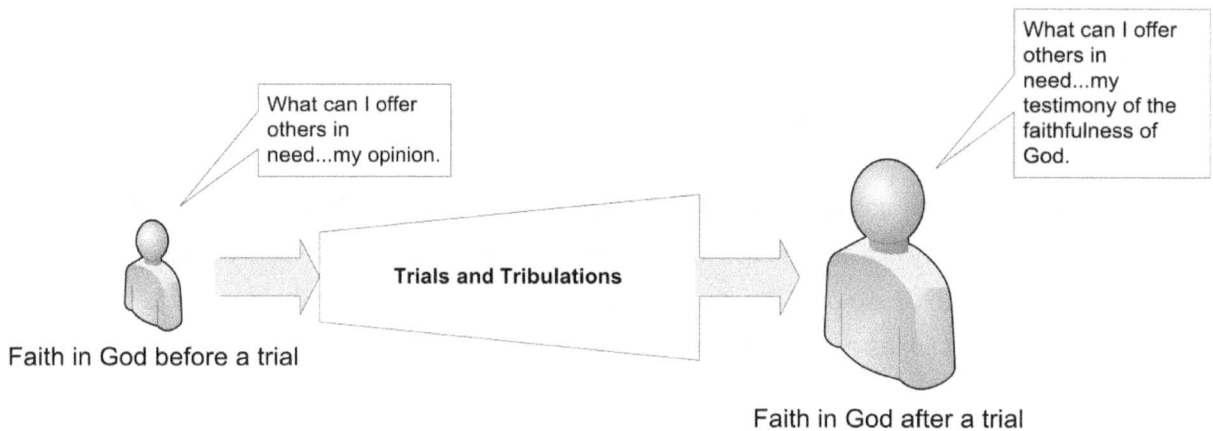

What can I offer others in need...my opinion.

What can I offer others in need...my testimony of the faithfulness of God.

Trials and Tribulations

Faith in God before a trial

Faith in God after a trial

Another reason is given for our trials in this chapter. Read 2 Corinthians 1:8 – 10. God wants us to rely "completely" on Him, not on our own strength. That's why some of our trials seem to be "beyond us"; the "heat" of the situation drives us to Him. What typically happens is that we get to the end of our resources, strength, and wisdom, and have nowhere to turn but towards God. Generally, the quicker we get there, the less heat we have to experience.

> *During your last trial, how quickly did it take for you to turn completely to the Lord? Immediately or after some time? Why do you think it takes some people so long to go to the Lord? Why do people sometimes try to find relief in a bottle of alcohol? Drugs? Gambling? Shopping? Eating? Does it provide lasting relief or momentary relief?*

Key Point: God Goes *ahead* of us in every situation we face.

Key Point: Sometimes our trials are the instruments God uses to help us mature spiritually. As a result, we become blessings for other people.

As additional emphasis of this point, read Exodus 13:20 – 22. The children of Israel had just left Egypt after the Passover. Notice how God manifested His presence to them, in pillars of fire and clouds. Verse 22 states that God was "in front" of the people. As His child, God will go before you.

A second reason not to fear is given in Deuteronomy 31:6 and in verse 8. God goes with us and will *never* leave us nor forsake us. When we meditate on that passage, we will realize that this has to be one of the most comforting truths we can have. You will *never* be alone; you will *always* have God with you; He will *never* forsake you. Let's break it down a little further.

In the King James Version verse 8 reads:

> "And the LORD, he it is that doth go before thee; he will be with thee, he will not fail thee, neither forsake thee: fear not, neither be dismayed."

The word "fail" comes from the word "raphah" which means:

- To sink
- To let go
- To drop
- To be silent
- To abandon

God will not let you sink, fall, or be silent. His love is confirmed by His actions, either in the circumstances, in you, or both.

Key Point: God won't let you go.

The word "forsake" comes from the word "'azab" which means:

- To depart from
- To leave behind
- To let alone

God will not leave you behind. To re-enforce this point, read Romans 8:35 – 39.

Key Point: Nothing can separate you from the love of God through Christ. God will not leave you behind.

Key Point: No matter what you are going through, God will not let you sink. He will not be silent; He will not abandon you. You will not be left alone. Therefore since the Creator of all things will never leave you, you have no reason to fear.

Re-enforcement

What's so good about God is that He will re-enforce our faith when we need it. In Joshua 1, Moses had died. Joshua was now in charge of the entire nation of Israel, probably between 2 to 4 million people. Joshua was an eye witness to how "troublesome" this new nation could be. He had witnessed the numerous times they wanted to stone Moses. Now he was in charge. But God spoke to him directly and re-enforced his faith. Read Joshua 1:1 – 9.

God again tells Joshua that He will never leave him nor forsake him. In addition He commands Joshua to be "strong and courageous". In verses 7 and 9, the word "strong" comes from the word "chazaq" which means:

- To be strong
- To be firm
- To grow stout
- To withstand

The word "courageous" (or courage, KJV) comes from the word "amats", which means:

- To be brave
- To be bold
- To be assured
- To be determined
- To confirm oneself

We are to walk with confidence and in a state of mind that we are assured of ourselves, because God is with us wherever we go (Joshua 1:9). Our confidence is not in ourselves, but in God, who is with us. That is why we should not fear.

Key Point: God is with us where ever we go. As a result, we can walk in confidence.

How To Make This Work

Now you might be saying, "Vic, this is all well and good; and I feel better now. But what about tomorrow? How do we live without fear after some time has passed, after we read these scriptures? " The only way I know is to "pray without ceasing" and to "meditate" on His Word. This is what I mean: On my way to work, I will say a prayer at the stoplight, praising God for the things He has recently done for me. Then at the next light, I will praise and thank God for what He has done for me in the past. I will be very specific in my prayer. Instead of saying, "Lord, thank you for everything you did for me yesterday", I would say, "Lord, thank you that you allowed me to miss that car that stopped suddenly in front of me. And Lord, thank you that my family was able to eat a good meal and spend some time together yesterday. And Lord, thank you that you allowed me to hear some encouraging words from my pastor yesterday that will help me address this situation at work. And Lord, ..." You get the point; I am very specific with my prayer. Then I will think about a scripture passage I read that morning and imagine how the people felt, and how God worked in their lives.

What am I doing by all this praying and mediating? I am flooding my mind with God-centered thoughts as opposed to the *imaginations* that cause me to fear. And I'm not simply substituting one thought for another; I am "*consuming*" my mind with the *Truth.* I don't want to give a "fearful imagination" any foothold in my mind.

Read Joshua 1:7 – 8. God commands Joshua how to be "strong and very courageous"…by focusing wholeheartedly on His Word. The power of the Word of God is what saves you, not your efforts. His Word is the key to our salvation. (That is why the Word became flesh - to be our salvation).

Summary

On the surface it may seem odd for God to tell us to "fear not"; fear comes so naturally at times. Also, a quick review of the daily news can make us fearful. But after understanding the reasons why we should not fear, it becomes clear – the Creator of the Universe loves us unconditionally and will never leave us. It's like His love is a thick, warm blanket that comforts us on a cold winter night. We can wrap ourselves in the comfort of his love and know that He will not turn His back on us; we won't fall. Better yet, He will go "ahead" of us and face any and every issue that comes before us. There is literally no reason to fear.

Notes:

Chapter 42: There Is Hope

Introduction

Trials and tribulations are a natural part of a believer's life. There may come certain seasons in our lives when tough times seem to last forever, or there is one trial right after another. When these times extend from days to weeks to years, it becomes more difficult to keep our focus on the Lord. We sometimes wonder if God has forsaken us. We think, "If He hasn't forsaken me, when am I ever going to get a break? I'm tired!"

This lesson is designed to help the believer maintain his/her hope; to realize that there is a reward for us if we endure to the end...not because we deserve it...but because He is faithful.

Scriptures Used In This Lesson

Job 1:1

Job 1:6 – 12

James 5:16

Job 2:1 – 10

Deuteronomy 32:4

Do You Feel Like Job?

During our Christian journey, we may experience a season of trials. Seasons, by definition, last for a period of time; they are not short in their duration. During one season, a friend once told me, "Vic, if anyone has gone through a 'Job-type' experience, it's been you." I thought to myself, "You know, he's right. It seems like bad news is coming at me from every angle – over a long period of time." Do you feel like Job sometimes? I did.

To get a better understanding of our "season of trials", we need to analyze certain passages in the book of Job. First of all Job was righteous. Read Job 1:1

> There was a man in the land of Uz, whose name was Job; and that man was perfect
> and upright, and one that feared God, and eschewed evil. (KJV)

The word "perfect" comes from the Hebrew word "tam" which means:

- One who is morally and ethically pure; having integrity
- Sound, wholesome

"Upright" comes from the Hebrew word "yashar", which means:

- Upright, just, level, pleasing, correct, righteous

When the Bible says that Job "eschewed evil" (English "eschewed" - Hebrew: "cuwr"), it means that he turned away from, or avoided evil.

Putting this together we can conclude that Job was a wholesome man of integrity who respected God, avoided evil, and was pleasing in His sight. The interesting point to note is that Job did not experience his trials because of anything he did; he did not lead a sinful lifestyle.

Key Point: Sometimes the trials you experience are *not* the result of any specific sin you have committed.

Key Point: God doesn't punish you over and over again for a sin you committed in the past from which you have repented. The blood of Jesus washes our sins away before God, allowing us to approach Him in confidence as children loved by their Father.

So what was going on in Job's life? What did he do wrong? The answer is, "Nothing." To discover the real answer, we need to read Job 1:6 – 12.

In this passage we see that God was "bragging" on Job in verse 8; He reaffirms the character of Job. Verses 9 – 11 reveal the "hidden war" that was being conducted without Job's knowledge. In essence Satan was saying that the only reason why Job was righteous and feared God was because God had blessed and protected Job. God said Job was righteous and a man of integrity, and Satan said he wasn't. Satan was telling God that He was wrong and rejected God's words.

The true battle in Job's life was between Satan and God. Satan was using Job to attack God's word and nature.

Key Point: Sometimes there is real spiritual warfare going on around you that can directly affect your life.

Spiritual Warfare

A natural question to this key point is: "How do I know if there is spiritual warfare going on that's affecting my life? How do I know what's going?"

Here are some key questions that will help answer that question:

- Are you actively involved in a ministry? A "ministry" is some work or service to which God has called you and it is affecting the lives of others in a positive way. If so, you are a threat to Satan.

- Are you "serious" about your personal relationship with God? Are you actively, earnestly seeking Him? Are you actively engaged in allowing Him to be Lord of your life? If so, you are a threat to Satan.

- Do you have a "powerful" prayer life? This prayer life is like the one described in the second half of James 5:16.

    The King James Version reads:

    …The effectual, fervent prayer of a righteous man availeth much.

    The verse contains words we don't use very much, but if we define "effectual", "fervent", and "availeth", we can gain this understanding of the verse:

    "Prayers that are effective, intense, heartfelt and without ceasing, have power that will be shown by extraordinary deeds."

    Can your prayer life (for the most part) be described in this manner? If so, you are a threat to Satan.

- Do you strive to live a life of integrity, like Job? Can others see Christ in the way you conduct your life? If so, you are a threat to Satan.

If you answered, "No." to all of the questions above, then chances are that there is no spiritual warfare in your life contributing to your season of trials. If you are not a real threat to Satan, the only reason he would declare war on you is to affect a godly person who is close to you. No military leader will waste resources on a non-threatening target. He will engage in warfare only on those targets that are a threat to him.

But if you answered, "Yes" to one or more of these questions, be aware that the battle has already started. The battleground may be in any one or more of the following areas:

- Your mind
- Your emotions
- Your finances
- Your body
- Your vocation
- Your family
- Your church or church members
- Your friends
- Your past
- Your ministry

Can you answer "Yes" to any of the questions above? If not, why? What is holding you back from being fully devoted to the Lord? Is fear one of the reasons? If so, why should you be afraid if you are fulfilling the will of God in your life?

More of The Same

Read Job 2:1 – 10. Verse 3 is very interesting. We can see that Job kept his integrity, even through the trials, as attested by God Himself. This is a lesson for us:

Key Point: It *is* possible to keep our integrity through our trials.

Do you know of someone who kept their integrity through a trial? How did they do it? What were the consequences of them keeping their integrity, i.e., how were they perceived afterwards? Do you know someone who did not keep their integrity during a trial? What were the consequences of them losing their integrity?

Satan dismisses Job's continued integrity in verse 4 and asserts that Job only maintains his integrity because his health has not been affected. God allowed Satan to affect Job's health and Satan "inflicted Job with painful sores" all over his body.

We need to keep in mind that Satan's primary attack was directed toward God; Job was just the object that Satan used to attempt to prove God wrong.

The Bridge To Hope

The key verses that serve as the bridge to Job's restoration are verses 1:22 and 2:9 – 10. Re-read those verses.

After losing all his children and wealth, verse 1:22 says that Job did not sin by *charging God with wrongdoing.* After losing his health and being encouraged to "curse God and die" by his wife, verse 2:10 said that Job did not sin *in what he said.*

Both of these verses declare that Job did not sin (i.e., separate himself from God) by accusing God of wrongdoing, or being unrighteous or unjust in *any* of His ways, including ways that allowed Satan to kill his children. These verses say a lot about our God. Read Deuteronomy 32:4.

The Word says in the NIV:

> He is the Rock, his works are perfect, and all his ways are just. A faithful God who does no wrong, upright and just is he. (NIV)

This verse is indicative of God's character, His nature, and His ways. To say anything contrary to this verse amounts to an attack on God Himself. This begs the question:

> How can a God who is righteous, faithful, and perfect allow Job's children to be killed, especially when Job routinely offered sacrifices to God for their sins (Job 1:5)?

More importantly we need to ask:

> How can God who is righteous, faithful, and perfect allow my child(ren) to be killed, or my spouse to die, or for my job to be eliminated, or my enemy at work/school to prevail over me?

If we are in the midst of spiritual warfare, like Job, the issue is bigger than us. Satan was attacking the very nature of God who rules and sustains the universe. If God is "flawed" in any way, then there is no need to serve Him; salvation is invalid; His commands don't have to be obeyed; He can't be fully trusted.

When we "stand" in the midst of spiritual warfare, we affirm God's righteousness. We affirm that He is holy and faithful and just. Our faithfulness to Him affirms His faithfulness. The enemy loses. Our faithfulness to Him establishes a bridge to our restoration.

Key Point: During a season of trials, in the midst of spiritual warfare, we may never know all the "Why's" of our troubles. Job didn't. But if we stand, God is true to reward us in this life and the one to come, because He is faithful.

Crossing the Bridge

Is there hope? Yes, yes and yes! There is hope. Read Job 42:7 – 17. Verse 7 indicates that God was not pleased with Job's friends because they did not speak what was right about the Lord, like Job did. They spoke error concerning His ways.

Ultimately God restored to Job twice as much wealth as he had before. God was not stingy; He restored *twice* as much as he had at first. This shows the true loving nature of our God. He also gave him ten more children and extended his life 140 years so that he could enjoy the fullness of all that He had provided.

Summary

Your season of trials may be due to spiritual warfare that's being engaged around you. If so, be encouraged – you're doing something right. You may be the object in the assault against the character of God. Stand firm and affirm His faithfulness and character. And watch what you say.

Notes:

_____

_____

_____

_____

_____

_____

_____

_____

_____

_____

_____

_____

_____

_____

_____

_____

_____

_____

_____

_____

_____

_____

_____

_____

_____

_____

_____

Psalm 37: A Psalm of Justice and Hope

Introduction

People have been doing wrong to each other since Cain and Abel. There has been a progressive separation from God, His ways, His fellowship, and His way of thinking. We've gotten to the point where we sometimes call what's good "bad", and what's bad "good". We see people "getting away with murder" and it seems like there's no real justice anymore. We sometimes wonder, "Where's God in all this? Why doesn't He just zap 'em with a lightening bolt or something?"

Well justice does come to evil people and there is hope for those who have been wronged. Psalm 37 is a psalm of justice and hope. If we can remember its instruction, it can keep us in right fellowship with God even in the midst of being wronged.

Scriptures Used In This Lesson

Psalm 37

First Things First

Verse 1 – Don't Fret

The first thing God tells us to do in the midst of someone's wrongdoing is, "Do not fret".

The verse reads:

> "Fret not yourself because of evildoers, neither be envious against those who work unrighteousness." (Amplified version)

"Fret" comes from the Hebrew word "charah" which means to be hot, furious, to burn with anger, to be incensed.

It's expected for us to be angry at wrong doing, but what God is telling us (commanding us) is to *not burn with a deep seated anger* because of those who do evil; not to get so enraged that you're out of control, and the anger *consumes* you. A consuming anger opens the door to bitterness of the heart.

Verse 8 states that fretting only leads to evil. Why do you think that's true?

Verse 2 tells us why we are not to fret.

> "For they shall soon be cut down like the grass, and wither as the green herb" (Amplified version)

Evil people will be repaid for their actions. But now you may wonder, how long is "soon"? Well, let's take a look and see how grass dies.

- There is a season when grass in a field is green and prospers. Then after a period of time, the season changes and it soon begins to wither and die. Winter always comes, no matter how hot and wet the summer gets. In winter, the grass can be easily cut; the season for its growth has ended. Evildoers sometimes experience a season where they are "high and mighty". They seem almost untouchable. And it appears like their dominance will never end. *But there is always a change of seasons.* A time will come where their power and influence will slip away and they will be cut down easily.

- Sometimes there's a drought during the season of growth. The grass may grow quickly in the spring, but the drought deprives the grass of what is vital for its life...water. Droughts are sometimes slow to overtake the grass, but when they come, the grass slowly; surely it withers and dies. Sometimes evildoers are deprived of what they crave the most. The thing which "got them to the top" and gave them their power, will be what brings them down. This type of downfall comes more quickly than the change of season, but has the same effect - they will wither and die.

- Sometimes there is a sudden disaster that overcomes the grass, like a fire or disease. Trouble has no favorites. Evildoers can enjoy long days of prosperity, and then all of a sudden, disaster strikes.

- And finally, there are times when the grass is immediately cut down. Just when it starts to get tall, it is mowed down. Sometimes it's best to cut the grass before it gets too tall. Otherwise it will be harder to handle later. There are times when God deals with the evildoer immediately. They are cut down before they have the opportunity to spread their brand of trouble.

The point is that there are at least four ways in which grass dies, all with a different timeframe. But all grass dies and can be easily cut down.

Key Point: God is just. He does not allow evildoers to go unpunished. Sometimes justice comes quickly and sometimes it comes after a season.

Name some incidents, historical or current, in which an injustice was done. Did the perpetrators go unpunished? Did they eventually "meet their Maker"?

But what are we to do in the meantime?

The next few verses provide clear instruction from the Lord.

v. 3 Trust in the Lord and do good...

v. 4 Delight yourself in the Lord...

v. 5 Commit your way to the Lord...

v. 7 Be still before the Lord and wait patiently for Him...

All of them say in effect, "Focus on the Lord, not on your circumstances or other people."

Key Point: In the midst of your being wronged, feeling down, angry, or troubled, focus on the Lord. This is not a suggestion, but a command.

"Trust" comes from the word "batach", which means to trust, be confident, to be sure, to be bold, to put confidence in, to make to hope. So to "trust" in the Lord means to be bold and have confidence in the Lord; to be sure about Him – not specifically how He will accomplish something, but in His character.

"Delight" comes from the word "anag", which means to be happy about, to take exquisite delight in, to make merry over. Delighting ourselves in the Lord means that He is our source of joy, not our circumstances. Circumstances change, but God does not.

"Commit" comes from the word "galal" which means to roll, commit to, to seek occasion. When we commit to the Lord, we "roll" His way, in effect. Like a boulder rolling down hill, we are to be committed to a direction towards Him.

To "be still and wait" comes from the word "damam", which means to rest, to quiet oneself, to be silent, to stand, still, to wait. This command is the hardest to follow sometimes, especially when we don't follow the previous three. As stated earlier, sometimes a "season" has to pass before evil people are "cut down". We may see it or we may not, but their time will come.

Which of the above commands is hardest for you to follow? Why?

Fortunately, God makes it easy on us. How? He provides promises of blessings for those who are obedient. Let's finish reading the verses:

3 Trust in the LORD and do good;

dwell in the land and enjoy safe pasture.

4 Delight yourself in the LORD

and he will give you the desires of your heart.

5 Commit your way to the LORD;

trust in him and he will do this:

6 He will make your righteousness shine like the dawn,

the justice of your cause like the noonday sun.

7 Be still before the LORD and wait patiently for him;

do not fret when men succeed in their ways,

when they carry out their wicked schemes. (NIV)

The remainder of the chapter follows the same pattern – clearly stated declarations of justice, with blessing promised to the righteous.

9 For evil men will be cut off,

but those who hope in the LORD will inherit the land.

Justice and hope in the same verse.

10 A little while, and the wicked will be no more;

though you look for them, they will not be found.

11 But the meek will inherit the land

and enjoy great peace.

Again, justice and hope. This pattern is continued throughout the Psalm.

Verses 25 – 28 have been especially encouraging to me over the years.

25 I was young and now I am old,

yet I have never seen the righteous forsaken

or their children begging bread.

26 They are always generous and lend freely;

> their children will be blessed.
>
> [27] Turn from evil and do good;
> then you will dwell in the land forever.
> [28] For the LORD loves the just
> and will not forsake his faithful ones.

So, no matter how bad things get, I *know* I will never be forsaken. His love for me won't allow it. That's what it means when the scriptures speak of His "steadfast love".

Two key points to remember during bad times are the following:

Key Point: Don't look at the bigness of your problem, but look at the bigness of your God.

Key Point: The pillars of fire and cloud never left Israel during their travel through the wilderness. In the same way, the Holy Spirit will never leave you.

Summary

I can't really express the concepts more clearly than the way they are presented in the Scriptures. The last two verses summarize the Psalm:

> [39] The salvation of the righteous comes from the LORD;
> he is their stronghold in time of trouble.
> [40] The LORD helps them and delivers them;
> he delivers them from the wicked and saves them,
> because they take refuge in him.

Notes:

Answers To Prayers

The purpose of this section is to assist in developing the realization that God "does" answer prayer. When documenting your requests, keep these things in mind:

- Is this request consistent with God's plan/purpose for my life?
- Can God be glorified through this request?
- Is this a need or desire?
- God will not grant a request that violates His word or principles.

Date: _____

Request: _____

_____

_____

Answer to Request: _____

_____

_____

Date: _____

Request: _____

_____

_____

Answer to Request: _____

_____

_____

Driven To Our Knees

Date: _____

Request: _____

_____

_____

Answer to Request: _____

_____

_____

Date: _____

Request: _____

_____

_____

Answer to Request: _____

_____

_____

Date: _____

Request: _____

_____

_____

Answer to Request: _____

_____

_____

Date: _____

Request: _____

_____

_____

Answer to Request: _____

_____

_____

Date: _____

Request: _____

_____

_____

Answer to Request: _____

_____

_____

Date: _____

Request: _____

_____

_____

Answer to Request: _____

_____

_____

Date: _____

Request: _____

_____

_____

Answer to Request: _____

_____

_____

Date: _____

Request: _____

_____

_____

Answer to Request: _____

_____

_____

Date: _____

Request: _____

_____

_____

Answer to Request: _____

_____

_____

Your Blessing Book

In this section, document the ways the Lord has blessed you. Over time, you will be encouraged as you read all that He has done in your life. Try this every day for thirty days. Please feel free to copy this page as many times as you need.

Date: _____

Blessing: _____

_____

_____

_____

Date: _____

Blessing: _____

_____

_____

_____

Date: _____

Blessing: _____

_____

_____

Date: _____

Blessing: _____

_____

_____

_____

Date: _____

Blessing: _____

_____

_____

_____

Date: _____

Blessing: _____

_____

_____

_____

Date: _____

Blessing: _____

_____

_____

_____

Date: _____

Blessing: _____

_____

_____

_____

Date: _____

Blessing: _____

_____

_____

_____

Date: _____

Blessing: _____

_____

_____

_____

Date: _____

Blessing: _____

_____

_____

_____

Date: _____

Blessing: _____

_____

_____

_____

Date: _____

Blessing: _____

_____

_____

_____

Date: _____

Blessing: _____

_____

_____

_____

Date: _____

Blessing: _____

_____

_____

_____

Date: _____

Blessing: _____

_____

_____

_____

Date: _____

Blessing: _____

_____

_____

_____

Date: _____

Blessing: _____

_____

_____

_____

Date: _____

Blessing: _____

_____

_____

_____

Date: _____

Blessing: _____

_____

_____

_____

Date: _____

Blessing: _____

_____

_____

_____